Theoretical Fables

Penn Studies in Contemporary American Fiction
A Series Edited by Emory Elliott, University of California at Riverside

A complete listing of the books in this series appears at the back of this volume

Theoretical Fables

The Pedagogical Dream in
Contemporary Latin American Fiction

Alicia Borinsky

UNIVERSITY OF PENNSYLVANIA PRESS

Philadelphia

Permission is acknowledged to reprint material from
published sources. These are listed following the
Index at the back of this volume.

Copyright © 1993 by the University of Pennsylvania Press
All rights reserved
Printed in the United States of America

Library of Congress Cataloging-in-Publication Data
Borinsky, Alicia.
  Theoretical fables : the pedagogical dream in contemporary Latin
American fiction / Alicia Borinsky.
      p.   cm. — (Penn studies in contemporary American fiction)
  Includes bibliographical references and index.
  ISBN 0-8122-3234-8
  1. Spanish American fiction—20th century—History and criticism.
2. Argentine fiction—20th century—History and criticism.
3. Literature—Philosophy.   I. Title.   II. Series.
PQ7552.N7B67   1993
863—dc20   93-26561
                                                            CIP

for Jeffrey,
Natalia, and Ezra

Contents

Preface ix

1. An Apprenticeship in Reading:
Macedonio Fernández 1

2. Taming the Reader:
Jorge Luis Borges 17

3. Intelligence and Its Neighbors:
Gabriel García Márquez 34

4. Literature as Risk:
Julio Cortázar 53

5. A Poetics of Misencounters:
Adolfo Bioy Casares 73

6. Is There Style Without Gender?
Manuel Puig 88

7. The Lucidity of Inaction:
María Luisa Bombal 104

8. Closing the Book—Dogspeech:
José Donoso 118

9. Overstaying My Welcome:
Conclusions 132

Bibliography 135

Index 143

Preface

"Maestro," teacher, was the word Jorge Luis Borges used to refer to Macedonio Fernández. Macedonio, an Argentine writer and philosopher, died in 1952 at age 77, relatively unknown to mainstream readers despite the profound mark he had left on a number of younger writers.[1] When I sat in Borges's classes on English and North American literatures at the University of Buenos Aires, the rediscovery of Macedonio had not yet taken place,[2] and listening to Borges talk about him[3] I felt that he was communicating a secret, a register for understanding his own thought, perhaps thought itself. "Maestro," of course, was said with reverence and humor, with no trace of the solemnity of the disciple acknowledging authority. When, years later, I found myself researching Macedonio's work and life and went to consult with Borges, he urged me to hurry and complete the project because it was important to "construct the myth of Macedonio." Frustrating as it was at the time, Borges's response was nevertheless illuminating because Macedonio, who thought of himself as a myth conceived by Borges and Ramón Gómez de la Serna,[4] was a seemingly inexhaustible source for metaphysical connections between what was written on the page and the ultimate goals reading might attain. Macedonio was "maestro," then, not only because *he* taught but because literature itself was viewed as a matrix for pedagogical efforts.

Contemporary Latin American fiction has attained a singular lucidity about the workings of language. Its self-reflexivity, its playful relationship to history and the everyday, frequently woven into extravagantly complicated plots, have led many to believe that an awareness of writing and reading as such is its main purpose. Although the dismantling of the illusions of realism, naturalism, and historicism figures among the effects produced by its reading, the haunting and disturbing energy of the major works of this period lies in their capacity to invoke, in disparate ways, a region not *beyond* literature, but *through* literature. The deferment of meaning, the questioning of the stability of the self with the attendant suspicion of the category of voice, and the dismissal of linear plots point toward something more than their own dismantling energy.

Macedonio was the most extreme and explicit—as well as the first—Latin American author to call the bluff of traditional novelistic discourse through a practice bent on overcoming and correcting its near-sightedness, but later developments proved that he would not be alone in his notion that the literary by itself was to be dismissed as the *merely* literary. In the work of all the writers assembled in this book—Macedonio Fernández, Jorge Luis Borges, Adolfo Bioy Casares, Gabriel García Márquez, María Luisa Bombal, José Donoso, Manuel Puig, and Julio Cortázar[5]—there is an urgency to make writing fulfill the promise of its mirages. Whether through history, a new noncausal perception of the world, a nostalgic feminine realm, or the abysses opened up by fear, their works ask us to perform a reading that would take into account literature's most destabilizing effects. And yet I refer to them as "theoretical fables."

"Theoretical" attempts to name the lucidity with which language works and the universalizing force that sustains it, as though we were presented each time with all-encompassing hypotheses about the nature of representation.[6] "Fables" refers to the fictional nature of what we read even as it suggests the effort to produce what in contemporary terms may be understood as a moral: not a clear-cut lesson to be followed but the uncovering of a path toward the intuition of its message. Theoretical fables, then, are written and received as post-theological and post-philosophical discourses, in which simulacra of philosophy, religion, theology, and history rehearse their elements as a joke in danger of reinscription.

The chapters in this book are arranged in a dialogue in which each of the readings contains, discusses, and completes or erodes another. The design is intended to engage the promise of the "theoretical" and make apparent the lucidity granted by a joint reading *within* fiction, since I have already assumed that it is through fiction that the aims of the theoretical are best fulfilled. I have not attempted to present an overview of contemporary Latin American fiction. The writers I discuss include established authors—Borges, García Márquez, Puig, Cortázar, Donoso—together with others whose works, for disparate reasons, have not yet been incorporated into the set of obligatory references. Adolfo Bioy Casares's writings have been too often read only in relationship to his literary collaborations with Borges, neglecting important considerations about the most specific aspects of his work. María

Luisa Bombal's vision is crucial to the understanding of a privileged passivity in literature, well beyond the impact that a reading of her fiction has on gender criticism. Macedonio Fernández's role in shaping the questions and texture of contemporary fiction will, I hope, become apparent to my readers and promote a new understanding of what is arguably the most creative fiction of the last decades.

As I interconnected the different chapters to make apparent the intensity of the vision present in each of the writers, I tried to highlight their will to persuade, the logic by which new, fragmented lessons are forged. It has become far too easy to find that literature and art celebrate their incapacity to render univocal meanings. In a sense, undecidability is the new happy ending of literary interpretation, a demagogy that relativizes individual interpretations of a given work even as it privileges critical discourse over "literature." This book has been written from a different perspective; the dialogue I establish is *within* fiction and, as a consequence, the text does not abound in critical notations although readers will find here pertinent historical and interpretive references.

Among the authors presented in this book are some to whom I am bound by friendship. The deaths of Jorge Luis Borges and Manuel Puig, two extremely different voices, played a role in my desire to complete this book and render testimony, to an extent, of one of their topics of conversation: an impatience with a certain kind of impoverishment as to what was perceived as literary. Borges, perhaps the most intellectual of readers, and Puig, the emotional, melodramatic delighter in poses, together gave me, in differing ways, two poles from which to rethink writing. These two authors are mutually exclusive but coexistent, and their loss prompted me to punctuate my readings of their work with personal recollection without losing sight of their impact on shaping the perspective from which I attempt to reveal the heterogeneity of the pedagogical in contemporary fiction. I am also indebted to Adolfo Bioy Casares for his friendship and the ease and rarity of his humor, and to José Donoso, whose reaction to what is perhaps the bleakest chapter in this book, the concluding part devoted to his work, gave reason to celebrate. The trust with which Adolfo de Obieta, Macedonio Fernández's son, granted me access to his father's archives enabled me to deepen an understanding that would have otherwise remained sketchy.

Not unlike others, but in a more secret layer, this book tells a story of encounters, cities, travels, chance, conversation. If the eloquence of the different literary visions evoked elicits participatory will in the readers, the dialogue I propose will have found its decisive point of departure.

Notes

1. Macedonio Fernández is himself the source of uncertainty about the date of his birth. In the few pages he devotes to what he entitles "Autobiography, Pose No. 1," he says, "The Universe or Reality and I were born on June 1, 1874." See Macedonio Fernández, "Autobiografía, Pose No. 1," in his *Papeles de recienvenido* (Buenos Aires: Centro Editor de América Latina, 1966), p. 115. In the same book, under the heading of "Argentine-Uruguayan Open Letter," he maintains: "[When I was born] I was in Buenos Aires; it was 1875: it was the year of the Revolution of 1874, just as afterwards we had a year for the revolution of 1890" (p. 49). Unless otherwise indicated, translations into English are mine.

2. The republication of his works started in 1966 with *Papeles de recienvenido*. Editorial Corregidor, in Buenos Aires, is currently bringing out in separate volumes his complete works, many of which had never been published. The University of Pittsburgh Press will be publishing a translation of his *Museo de la novela de la Eterna* in the near future.

3. Although the subject of the course was different, Borges would digress into recollections of conversations; those with Macedonio Fernández were ones evoked most frequently.

4. Borges, much younger than Macedonio, was thought of by the older writer as a *lector fantástico,* a fantastic reader who would make the project of a new kind of writing possible. The admiration that Borges had for him seemed to Macedonio to stem from Borges's own capacities for the fantastic. Ramón Gómez de la Serna, on the other hand, was a contemporary of Macedonio's, and their correspondence is a testimony to the admiration that Macedonio felt for him. When Gómez de la Serna published a flattering literary portrait of Macedonio, the latter's humorous response—in a letter—was that he would go into seclusion so as not to disappoint anyone with his presence. Macedonio's correspondence is an excellent source for documenting the quality of these literary friendships. See Macedonio Fernández, *Epistolario* (Buenos Aires: Editorial Corregidor, 1991).

5. I have not attempted to offer regional coverage. My reading tends to emphasize departures from local concerns which, in turn, might paradoxically illuminate local characteristics, as Borges has pointed out frequently in his thoughts about the relationship between the narrowly regional and the universal.

6. In this sense, my concerns intersect with those of literary theorists; in this book, though, I try to present fiction as the locus from which to elicit the theoretical. In spite of the Derridean and poststructuralist posture that encompasses all written representation as fictional, the preferred texts for discussion have become essays, with fiction and poetry taking a secondary position.

Aquí viven los héroes del snobismo (o los pensionistas de un manicomio abandonado). Sin espectadores—o soy el público previsto desde el comienzo—, para ser originales cruzan el límite de comodidad soportable, desafían la muerte.

—Adolfo Bioy Casares, *La invención de Morel*

Chapter 1
An Apprenticeship in Reading: Macedonio Fernández

In 1922 Macedonio Fernández wrote *Adriana Buenos Aires: The Last Bad Novel*.[1] He revised it in 1938, adding some chapters and taking out clues that might reveal its contemporary references. Thus the names of César and Santiago Dabove, which appeared throughout the 1922 text, were replaced with their initials. Adolfo de Obieta conjectures that *Adriana Buenos Aires* may have been part of Macedonio's plan for launching himself as a candidate for the Argentine presidency.[2]

If the role that this novel could have played in the 1927 political campaign now seems remote and dubious, an undeniable proselytism of a different order emerges. Macedonio wanted *Adriana Buenos Aires: The Last Bad Novel* to be published and sold under its complete title together with *Museum of the Novel of the Eternal: The First Good Novel*.[3] The two works, antagonistic twins, would serve the purpose of delivering a lesson about literature and the world to the public.

The merely aesthetic appears here as a trivializing category, in relationship to a truth that may be glimpsed from the reading of a truly bad piece of literature. In a dedication written by Macedonio, addressed to Alberto Hidalgo and quoted in the 1974 edition of *Adriana Buenos Aires*, we read:

To Alberto Hidalgo: And because he never doubted that I would compose the worst novel in its genre, given my unequivocal gifts and my strict and repeated promises (. .) The only real benefactors of national literatures are those who mortify it with the truth.[4]

Alberto Hidalgo's response—"I expected it, this is not the only bad thing you have been able to complete"—suggests the irony of the project but also the seriousness with which a literature of pedagogical purposes is viewed by both writers.

Adriana Buenos Aires is, according to Macedonio, the very model of a bad piece of literature. It has a plot, intrigue, sex, and money, all in a familiar and flat context. Its characters are portrayed as dependent on their practical circumstances. Readers become integrated into an anecdotal world said to have affinities with that of their own neighborhoods and needs.

The boarding house, frequently used as a device for the introduction of lower middle class and middle class characters in Latin American fiction, is the chosen theater for the exchanges from which the lessons of *Adriana Buenos Aires* are to be derived. The narrator explains to us his relationship with one of his friends, with whom he feels a strong bond:

> Soon he would sit in my room for hours so that he could know everything about me and tell me everything about himself. Whenever he stayed in the boarding house, he was wherever I was. For weeks we would barely say hello to each other: I was afraid he was putting on airs, he was the only wealthy one there; he would flee from any new relationship and, used to the comradeship of students, people "of a certain age" looked much older than they actually were to him and he did not trust them. (. .) He was never put on edge by the landlady's four daughters or by the various single women and ladies who would come and go in the boarding house; meanwhile half a dozen intrigues would be going on in the house, whispers here, tiptoeings at night, a securely closed room that nobody would enter, while one door had just been closed in another room and a bit farther, in a darkened chamber, a light would go on for a minute and then be off. (p. 77)

The friend represents a privileged relationship to the world of the boarding house. Holding the promise of stories behind each door, that institution is a treasure chest for a literature of intrigue. The narrator's friend, we are told, is wealthy enough to be above the pettiness of poverty; he is aloof and he feels no need to interact with the inhabitants of the boarding house.

The narrator praises his relationship to this character with a middle class cliché in emphasizing that, as far as the others are concerned, his attitude is one of aristocratic detachment. He is there but he is not truly interested. He is able to observe that world without being infused with the vulgarity emanating from it. What do narrator and friend talk about? "He would sit in my room for hours so that he could know everything about me and tell me everything about himself." The hypothesis is one of interiority: they exchange confidences and their selves come together through autobiographical chats. But the bond of their friendship is unstable; sometimes they barely say hello to one another. The explanation is their difference in age, because the friend does not trust people "of a certain age." The implicit youth granted to this friend suggests that the anxiety caused by his occasionally faint greetings denotes a relationship to time: an older man's fear of being left aside and the consequent sense that only the young are in a position to take control and decide who will survive in the collective imagination.

The boarding house partakes of a contemptible realm, whereas the friendship based on the autobiographical suggests that there is a necessary but unstable pact grounding the perception of that world. Thus *The Last Bad Novel* suggests through its anecdotes the implicit entities that make it possible. The narrator suffers from an illusion that is at the root of various naturalistic and realistic readings: he is in love with Adriana, a vulnerable character whose problems are a demonstration of some of society's ills as well as testimonies to a lover's capacity for abnegation and jealousy in the reorganization of the world required by his all-consuming passion.

Adriana Buenos Aires reshuffles the alternatives emerging from these characteristics by emphasizing the tension felt by the narrator due to his desire for Adriana. Adriana is the parameter according to which he measures his own reactions to other characters. His love for her is an interpretative system and a code of behavior for him. He tells the reader that Adriana is also fervently desired by others, thus granting to his sense of her the quality of an intersubjective truth:

This thought should be painful to me; I wished for Adriana to inspire many faithful loves and attachments. But a sick man's passion, a man whose company was even a risk for Adriana's mental health at the moment, and a further risk of violences and assaults perhaps later on, was a different case. And since that passion though beautiful did not have the dignity of a high form of love as could be inferred from that memorable reaction of Adriana's on the night of Adolfo's return, and since I had not been honest in my behavior toward him, I did not need to be that way now, when it was a question of Adriana, because whether I crossed paths with Adriana before or after him, and even if our friendship had come to be before our knowledge of that fact, I firmly believe that there is no moral theory that could argue for limitations governing my free actions toward the achievement of a love. (pp. 210–11)

The desire of the narrator and other characters in the novel finds its predicate in Adriana. Enigmatic, beautiful, long suffering, she embodies elements that make it possible and necessary to theorize about life and ethics. The ethics she inspires is rooted in immediate existence; Adriana and the rest of the characters in this novel are decidedly grounded in this world.

Complications, disdainful turns, fatherless children, illicit love affairs, tragic deaths, lives that take place within view of participatory gazes. *Adriana Buenos Aires* intends to conclude with this kind of literature by convincing us that our attachment to its illusions is nefarious and by advancing the hypothesis that its plots are merely a protracted lie.

The persona of the author is ubiquitous. He tells us in the beginning how to read the novel so that we may be protected from the mirages provoked by fiction. The narrator, in love with Adriana, changes his place at times with an implicit reader who also desires her. The author, signed "M. F.," is a reminder of the pedagogical goal of the experiment. Surrounded by a group of literary friends, he creates a certain bustle around it.[5] In the first pages of the novel we read quotations of alleged opinions attributed to Alberto Hidalgo, Jorge Luis Borges, Francisco Luis Bernárdez, and Raúl Scalabrini Ortiz which support the notion that *Adriana Buenos Aires* is indeed an extremely bad and perhaps—here opinion varies—a definitive work. Borges's sentiment is exemplary of what would become his own stand regarding literature and repetition as years went by: "If it belongs to the bad genre I've been promised, it will not be the last" (p. 15).

The consensus about the novel presented by Macedonio tends to curb hopes without blunting the acuteness of Macedonio's sense of what constitutes good and bad literature. Thus the novel is seen as a humorous instrument of enlightenment; it teaches not because it is good but rather because of the reverse. It does not teach by itself but does so together with its antagonistic twin, *Museum of the Novel of the Eternal*.

The transmission of the novel's wisdom is conceived here as learning through an example of badness, a shock that incites readers to work against the grain of what they read, to rebel and reject, thereby entering into a hard apprenticeship. The tone is deliberately apocalyptic: this will be the last bad novel. With a somewhat naive optimism, Macedonio dreamt of a future of awareness through literature, a reconsideration of the aesthetic that would not allow a relapse into acknowledged errors. Loving Adriana is thus a major equivocation. The literature that produces her induces infatuations similar to the one experienced by the novel's narrator; by following that road we face the need to compromise and accept a notion of the self as that which can be autobiographed and a sense of time as occurring in a linear sequence, leading to death.

The Flip Side

With dogged determination and a will to coherence that frequently borders on the philosophical, Macedonio Fernández next undertook the task of writing what he called "the first good novel" in *Museum of the*

Novel of the Eternal. His explicit purpose is to theorize and produce the first example of this genre yet without readers or writers. In that sense, *Museum of the Novel of the Eternal* is his most ambitious work, since in others the claims are more restrained; *No toda es vigilia la de los ojos abiertos* is philosophical and *Papeles de Recienvenido* is an exercise in humor.

Macedonio proposes a doubling for the practice of reading that is coupled with a doubling in the writing itself: theory and practice of the novel are combined; the one unfolds so that it may criticize the other even while illuminating it. We are given a text that wills the literal as slippage in a game that needs the reader's unfailing complicity. The concrete locale for this complicity is *Adriana Buenos Aires*'s twin, a work composed of fifty-six anticipatory and theorizing moments referred to as prologues, twenty chapters, four final sections, and a dedication. Whereas *Adriana Buenos Aires* invited us to share in a chronological temporality consisting of mardi gras celebrations, deaths, and age differences, the web created by "the first good novel" wants us to *forget* the moment in which its pages were produced and relinquish the calendar. The dialogue it establishes with the reader suggests that deferment is more important for the understanding of what we call meaning than its illusionary and momentary incarnations.

Prefiguring the thought of the French writer Maurice Blanchot, but with a sense of humor, Macedonio Fernández advocates a literature that would be a kind of tabula rasa of history, a primal scene of interlocution. A context may be inferred, nevertheless, for *Museum of the Novel of the Eternal* from the critical stands with which Macedonio supports his project.

In "Toward a Theory of Humoristics"[6] Macedonio attempts a critique of realistic humor that is at once naive and illuminating. He advances his own punning against the kinds of humor he derides (notably Freud's examples and treatments of jokes, among others) as well as his certitudes about the workings of the uncanny, and a total confidence in the practice of the absurd, which he calls, with a capital letter, "Ilógica" Macedonio uses the same methodology for his scrutiny of humor in this essay as in his prescriptive understanding of the "good" novel. It involves something of a lesson to the reader in the hope that the generous humor of the absurd may be realized and displace the kind of selfish, lying jokes that keep him in the pettiest of domains. That kind of humor builds illusions every bit as contemptible as those elicited by *Adriana Buenos Aires*.

The archetypal reader of *Adriana Buenos Aires* is someone who reads in a linear manner, wishing to resolve the anxieties produced by the plot; *Museum of the Novel of the Eternal* is appalled by the reader's existence and speaks to his or her idiosyncrasies in one of its many prologues:

> I, who never believed in the existence of the Linear Reader and who was more in the right when I believed that I would find for my novel the only Linear Reader in existence, the one who would ruin and give away all my tricks, typical of a weak and repetitive writer confident in the fact that his incompletenesses would be swept away, unnoticed. If in fact you are wandering in my book, I know I have no hope left. (p. 112)

Although it is true that this author wants to teach, his persona is not that of the infallible master with submissive disciples; on the contrary, this author puts himself in his readers' hands and conveys to them his desire to be selective at the same time that he lets them know his own weaknesses. Thus the Linear Reader will realize that there are repetitions in the novel elicited by its pedagogical effort to the extent that he approaches its reading as though it worked like a traditional plot. The author foresees that the result of such a misunderstanding will be a refusal of the novel.

The ideal reader sought in *Museum of the Novel of the Eternal* is the opposite of the linear one; the former is called the "Skipping Reader," *Lector Salteado*. The reappearance in later Latin American novels of the distinction between two kinds of readers is striking. The most salient example is, no doubt, in Cortázar's *Hopscotch,* as well as in his sense of the permutations necessary for an adequate reading of his *62: A Model Kit*. Macedonio dedicates his novel to the *Lector Salteado*:

> I take shelter in the Skipping Reader. Here you are, you have read my whole novel without realizing it, you have turned into a Linear Reader unknowingly since I have told you everything in a dispersed way before the novel. The Skipping Reader is the one who is most at risk of reading linearly with me. I wanted to distract you, I did not want to correct you because, on the contrary, you are the wise reader since you practice an intermittent reading, which is the one that makes the most profound impression according to my theory that the characters and events that are merely suggested and left unfinished are those that stay the most in one's memory.
>
> I dedicate my novel to you, Skipping Reader; you will be grateful to me for a new sensation: reading linearly. The Linear Reader, on the contrary will have the sensation of a new way of skipping: following an Author who skips. (pp. 111–12)

Reader-writer, writer-reader, Macedonio produced a body of work that became readable years after its inception thanks to a literature that, emerging from the same matrix, gave life to its principles. It is now hard to recreate the polemical energy that drove Macedonio when he wrote his fiercely anti-realistic[7] pages. The isolation with which he wanted to cloak his persona as a writer is lost for us. In what cannot but be an act of *recognition* we read *Museum of the Novel of the Eternal* as it appears to us, intimately woven into the literature that followed.

For Macedonio, though, the feeling was the solitude of inaugurating something new:

And so came the time of my promising my novel and I would be reassured in the realization that people continued reading bad literature—for which I must thank the bad authors—and hoping for the good one—for which they must be grateful to me: we might say that we have cooperated but we shall not part radically when I begin. The only sensitive point is that since the new novelistic work is very good, one does not yet know when it will come to be. (pp. 108–9)

Macedonio's celebration of eccentricity and the transforming power of writing reveals his affinities with some of the avant-garde writers of his time, in particular with Vicente Huidobro in his manifesto phase,[8] although for Huidobro the changes could only be effected through the invention of new and surprising poetic images. The new literature conceived by Macedonio was, perhaps against his own will, an aristocratic genre par excellence, predicated against the tyranny of realism with its preferences for consensus building and common sense. In favoring uncertainty Macedonio was trying not merely to confuse readers but also to allow them into a realm forbidden to those clinging to the limitations of their own perceptions:

Let us build a spiral so twisted that even the wind would tire circulating inside it and would emerge from it dizzy, forgetting where it was going; let us build a novel just like it, one that would not be for once a clear, faithful realistic copy. Either Art does not matter or it has nothing to do with Reality; only thus does it become real itself in very much the same way that the different parts of Reality are not copies of one another. (p. 109)

Unlike Vicente Huidobro, Macedonio did not insist on the idea that "the different parts of Reality are not copies of one another" to support his sense of the literature he was founding. Whereas Huidobro's "Creacionismo" departed from that intuition to invent a literature imitative of the productive energy of nature rather than its individual products, for Macedonio the essential issue was one of ethical import. He based his criticism of that school on one of its own favorite concepts:

All realism in Art appears to have been borne out of the random fact that there are mirroring matters in the world with the result that store attendants thought of literature, that is to say of making copies. And what we call literature seems to be the work of an obsessive mirror salesman who lets himself into people's houses, pressuring them to predicate their own missions on mirrors, not things. How many moments of our lives have scenes, plots, characters? The mirror-work of art calls itself realistic but it intercepts our view of reality with a copy. (p. 109)

What would a literature that would not intercept reality be like? Is Macedonio's proposal for a literature that bites its own tail? What would be its function?

Macedonio is not concerned with realism's dependence on extraliterary elements; he is against its capacity for deception, its functioning simultaneously as art and as a transparent rendering of something behind it, with the result that its artistic nature is obscured. Thus there is a double masking: words and things lie about their own nature. Macedonio advocates an ideal nakedness for the named and the naming, a self-exposure, an awareness of what lies behind and beyond. His critique of realism is done in the name of truth; although Macedonio sometimes sounds as though he were a South American precursor of the reflections that are later found in deconstruction's efforts to dismantle Western metaphysics, his vision is different, even opposite. No more metaphysical than grasping onto notions of truth, Macedonio's authenticity is expressed without apologies:

The present ease in writing makes for the scarcity of the readable and has even done away with the annoying need for readers: one writes for artistic fruition and, at the most, for knowing the opinion of critics. Sincerely this change is beautiful; it is art for art's sake and art for criticism's sake. The horrible art and the accumulations of glory of the past, which will always exist, are due to the sound of the languages and to the existence of the public; left without public, declamatory calamities would not be the end of all art. (p. 45)

"The horrible art . . . of the past" implies a celebration of the present through the intuition of a future offering more intelligent and higher artistic works. Macedonio's work is genuinely optimistic, naively bent on the belief that artistic changes are moments in an ever closer relationship to an ultimate truth. The public he thinks is about to disappear is the readership of "bad novels" as exemplified by *Adriana Buenos Aires*; the new one constitutes the promise of a future for literature.

In rereading Macedonio's beliefs, one has the impression that he was writing in all innocence of affinities between the historical and the literary; his declarations are supported by broad views that extend into art history, literature, and philosophy, sometimes in one and the same paragraph. He was an impatient evaluator:

Literature would consist only of art and many more beautiful works: three or four Cervantes, only Quixote without the tales, Quevedo the humorist and poet of passion without the moralistic oratory, several Gómez de la Serna. Free from the horror of a Calderón, prince of falsetto, which is the absence of feeling and it is all bad taste, of a Góngora sometimes, the one of "estos, Fabio, ay dolor!" we would be happily left with only a first part of Faust and, in compensation, several Poes, several Bovarys with their sad suffering of loveless appetite, contemptible and cruel, and that other wounding absurdity: the lyricism of Hamlet's pain which convinces and creates sympathy in spite of the false psychology behind it. Free from Ibsen's scientized realism, one of Zola's victims, and, in turn, this artist dismantled by sociology and hereditary theory and pathology, instead of a dozen masterpieces we would have a hundred of intrinsic artistic truth, not copies of reality. And typically literary, of Prose, not of didacticism or words put to music (meter, rhyme, sound) or written painting, descriptions. (p. 45)

Macedonio's self-assuredness allows him to marginalize himself at the same time that he presents himself as an omnipotent critic of his culture. But in offering this succinct history of Western culture in *Museum of the Novel of the Eternal* he is doing much more than trying to destabilize the complacent categories that make up the accepted canon. His refusal is above all an effort geared toward the invention of a new register for his own work by eliminating that which *it is not*.

The brush strokes by which some authors are praised and others condemned constitute a genealogy of *Museum of the Novel of the Eternal*. The works being evoked are there so that the readers may infer what *Museum of the Novel of the Eternal* allows them to read and enjoy: it is possible to believe in Bovary and Don Quixote, to embrace Poe and Gómez de la Serna. Although we would be hard put to find a page in Macedonio's prose containing echoes of Poe, we find him here as part of a family portrait from which Calderón and the Cervantes of the "tales" have been expelled. The lineage that Macedonio has invoked for himself goes beyond the evocation of particular masterpieces: it wills itself as an exercise in reading as a generous tinkering with tradition.

Macedonio's radical discontent with established opinion regarding the quality of literature is evident in his forgetting the details of some of these works, the ease with which he rejects some cultural monuments, and the faithful eagerness with which he erects others, such as in the case of Gómez de la Serna. Reading is for him a most passionate endeavor, one that, according to the promise of *Museum of the Novel of the Eternal,* may take its practitioners into the realm of immortality. Thus realism, the sinister twin that confuses readers, is to be dismissed—if not for its bad taste, then for its promotion of laziness and deceit. In spite of Macedonio's explicit positions against didacticism, his condemnation of realism is declared in the name of teaching a good lesson through literature, thereby denouncing its opposite.

The Privilege of Stumbling onto Eternity

Borges wrote about Macedonio and liked to talk about him. He had been a "maestro" for him, he said. It was his dual practice of jokes and metaphysics that caught Borges's imagination at a time when Borges was young and a participant in the active intellectual life of Buenos Aires cafés, where Macedonio was a central figure.[8] Macedonio and Borges corresponded and conversed with each other. The traces of Macedonio's presence in the works of Borges are explicit; in "Dialogue About a Dialogue" by Borges we find a revealing evocation of Macedonio:

> A—Distracted and thinking about immortality we had allowed it to get dark without turning on the lights. We could not see our faces. With an indifference and a sweetness more persuasive than his fervor, Macedonio's voice reiterated that the soul is immortal. He assured me that the death of the body is totally insignificant and that dying has to be the most insignificant event to happen to anybody. I played with Macedonio's razor; I opened it and closed it. A neighboring accordion played incessantly "La Cumparsita," that consternated triviality that pleases many people just because they were told the lie that it is very old. . . . I proposed to Macedonio that we both commit suicide so that we could continue our discussion without intrusions.
>
> Z—(mockingly) But I suspect that in the end you did not dare.
>
> A—(already in utter mysticism) Frankly, I do not remember if we committed suicide on that night.[9] (p. 13)

Borges, the realization of Macedonio's dream of a fantastic reader of his literature, rehearses the literality of the project: it does not matter whether they committed suicide. The temporal reality of the project is to be ignored because in this conversation about a conversation, as the letters A and Z speak to each other, they presuppose and render unnecessary all the other letters between them. If the denial of actual death in this text appears with a humorous wink, the joke points out a concept that was crucial to an understanding of the metaphysical basis for Macedonio's critique of realism.

The *truth* that Macedonio was seeking was accessible through what he called "un tropezón conciencial," a stumbling of consciousness, whereby readers would abandon their belief in their individual identities in order to recognize themselves in another realm, which Macedonio named "almismo ayoico"—a selfless soulness. The "almismo ayoico," a stage beyond the individual self, is explained in metaphysical detail in *No toda es vigilia la de los ojos abiertos*[10] as well as in some sections of *Papeles de Recienvenido*;[11] it is a privileged state accessible through literature. According to Macedonio, the power of antirealistic literature is such that in denying readers the possibility of projecting themselves into other characters and by instead focusing intensely on the unreality of literature—on writing itself, which Macedonio calls "el Pensar," the act of thinking—it would allow them to experience the dismantling of their very selves.

Once the state of "almismo ayoico" is reached and the individual self has been truly dismantled *on an experiential level,* death is revealed to be an impossibility since, in Macedonio's view, it presupposes belief in the individual self. Borges's text recovers for us the way in which Macedonio referred to death as trivial insofar as it reaffirmed notions of the self he was intent on dispelling. Mockery of death in Borges is coupled with a mockery of the mockery of death; Macedonio, however, never subjected his "almismo ayoico" to the dismantling effects of humor. It remained one of the stable categories sustaining his sense of the purpose underlying the renewal of literature.

Nevertheless, Macedonio was a fervent humorist. It is through humor, he suggested, that the "tropezón conciencial" would allow readers to take the leap away from their individual selves. Years later, Cortázar would feature a photograph of the old Macedonio, with his long white beard, in his book of miscellany, *Around the Day in Eighty Worlds*;[12] Macedonio's sense of the importance of humor as a transformative tool reemerges in both Borges and Cortázar. Free from the paralyzing effects of Macedonio's proselytism, some of their works become puzzling realizations of his projects.

How to Read and Write the "Good Novel"

A great part of *Museum of the Novel of the Eternal* is a kind of instruction manual that shows the steps to be followed in helping "the first good novel" come to life. Time and again Macedonio derides mimetic characters ("personajes-copia"), accusing them of inducing a state of hallucination in the reader:

I want the reader to be always aware of the fact that he is reading a novel and not witnessing a living [*un vivir*], not seeing a life [*una vida*]. I will have lost, not won over a reader, the moment he falls into a hallucination, that ignominy of Art.(p. 39)

The belief in the existence of fictional characters is portrayed as favoring a pathological approach to reading, a hallucination that keeps the reader locked into a misguided belief in the existence of his personal self. Macedonio's aesthetical antihumanism is idiosyncratic; it is formulated as a victorious struggle against death, an intrusion in the sequential narrative we call destiny. Macedonio's contempt for individualistic common sense psychology is taken up by Cortázar's fictive author

Morelli[13] in *Hopscotch,* this time, though, without any illusion of attaining immortality.

What would a character who would not want to provoke hallucinations in us be like? One of Macedonio's strategies is a practice of incongruity, found as a device in other writers of his time, such as Huidobro, but with a different slant. The only other writer who approximated Macedonio's literature in this regard, according to Macedonio himself, was Ramón Gómez de la Serna. Their correspondence[14] is testimony to a shared sense of a new literature in the future consisting of incongruous characters and situations that required, as a counterpart, an ideal reader. The detailed discussions between Macedonio and Gómez de la Serna about the latter's "novelas de la nebulosa" (novels of the nebula) and Macedonio's own theory of the novel provide an unusual opportunity to see the degree of specificity with which narrative devices are aligned with metaphysical consequences for both writers:

> But I have already said, or I shall say it later on, that I employ every device, including incongruity, to defy verisimilitude, the plausibly puerile, with the artistic, and I point out and justify each of them. It is a more honest and harder task that I undertake for the public than the overused and comfortable one of introducing madmen in novels.[15] (p. 66)

The notion of honesty in a hard task being performed for the public delineates two poles for art seen as an interlocutionary system: author and reader have tasks to perform and must approach them with the right ethical stand. The persona of the author acquires messianic overtones in *Museum of the Novel of the Eternal*; he is able to sweep readers away from the imposition of death, to teach them how to go beyond their individual selves and train them to effectively perform the "tropezón conciencial"—the stumbling of conscience. In suggesting all these functions for the author, Macedonio oscillates between feelings of omnipotence and humility. *Museum of the Novel of the Eternal* closes with the thought that the author was perhaps unable to bring his project to completion.

Macedonio's ideal reader was at once a hypothesis and a concrete reality. He is invoked constantly as a virtuality in *Museum of the Novel of the Eternal* and by name, concretely, in *Adriana Buenos Aires*. A gallery of readers traverses the pages of *Museum of the Novel of the Eternal*, some of them street characters portrayed with their tics, preferences, and anxieties about not having enough time, others acknowledged but dismissed from the beginning. Among those dismissed are Pedro Corto, "who wanted to read the novel beforehand to see whether he would like to be part of it" (p. 78), and Nicolasa Moreno, "who gladly agreed to participate provided her role allowed her to get out of the novel from time to time to check whether some milk she had put to boil was not overflowing"; the reasons for their dismissal are clearly purist: they are not committed to the novel with true disinterest (Pedro Corto) or they are too compromised by extraliterary reality (Nicolasa Moreno).

The best reader willed for itself by the novel is as messianic as the persona of the author himself. Through this reader the future of literature will be possible; the transgressiveness of the novel will acquire meaning and a realm of immortality will be instituted by literature as the result of the pact induced by the novel.

Macedonio has been reclaimed as a precursor by writers who view the novel as a hospitable genre, capable of incorporating in its unstable texture the heterogeneity stemming from its being a genre *in between* others, uncompromisingly free from literary convention. Paradoxically, Macedonio's attempt tends toward the achievement of a certain purity for the novel. It is, of course, a most idiosyncratic sort of purity. *Museum of the Novel of the Eternal* alternates between the genres of the novel, the essay, the joke, and poetry, but the purity it demands of itself resides in its antihallucinatory program rather than in the achievement of any given format. The destabilizing rhythm of its reading is a strategy for keeping readers alert, thereby forbidding the kind of complacency that would hinder their taking the spiritual leap that Macedonio's writing was intended to inspire.

Macedonio's explicit condemnations of didacticism in literature sprang from the contempt in which he held patronizing writers. His own attempt is pedagogical but requires the confusion of the categories of teacher and disciple at every turn. Only then may the literary past be reconsidered and the characters of *Museum of the Novel of the Eternal* fulfill, through the awkwardness of their invented names, the task of being vehicles for a "beyond" of literature.

Ideal Readers

Leopoldo Marechal's *Adán Buenosayres*[16] offers through its character Samuel Tesler, a philosopher and conversationalist, a fresh and critical view of Macedonio's project.

Samuel let out a malevolent bit of laughter and added: "What I can't understand is how our great Macedonio, living in Buenos Aires, could come to this surprising metaphysical conclusion: 'The world is an *almismo ayoico*.' God forgive his neologisms! As for myself, under the same circumstances, I would have arrived at another, very different one."—"And what is that?"—asked the guest—"At the following one, round, musical, and meaningful: 'The world is a *yoísmo al pedo.*'" (pp. 53–54)

Tesler's correction of Macedonio's assessment is no less metaphysical; "yoísmo al pedo"—a neologism that does as much violence to the ear as "almismo ayoico"—could be translated as "a farting self-centerdness." Following in Macedonio's footsteps, Tesler turns around and dismantles his system of interpretation by asserting the exact opposite of its founding presuppositions. Macedonio traverses Marechal's *Adán Buenosayres* as the metaphysical spirit in a city that, nevertheless, mocks his attempts at denaturalization of a language that he manipulated so well—although apologetically—in *Adriana Buenos Aires*. Tesler is both a philosophical and a physiological character and, in a gesture that may well be Nicolasa's and Pedro's revenge, he includes Macedonio in the novel as joke. But the architectural freedom of *Adán Buenosayres*, the insistence on self-reflexivity, and the frequent demands for the reader's complicity signal that its relationship to *Museum of the Novel of the Eternal* extends much farther than the mere literary revenge exercised by the characters dismissed from Macedonio's book because of their lack of faithfulness to the project.

Although Cortázar's playful strategies against common sense are to be understood as part of the heritage of Alfred Jarry and Dada, his novelistic practice reintroduces us to Macedonio, in particular with respect to the organization and resolutely antipsychological program informing *62: A Model Kit*. The reading required by *62: A Model Kit* puts into practice Macedonio's project of a novel made up of chapters that would be metaphors of each other, in an allusive, nonhierarchical chain. Whereas *Museum of the Novel of the Eternal* tries to perform the metaphorical project it suggests, the proposal implied in Cortázar's *62: A Model Kit* is quite different from the novel's own methods. They are the meanderings of desire and the terrors of a memory that is both private and collective.

Among the reader-writers invited by *Museum of the Novel of the Eternal*, Borges is no doubt the one who has attempted the most to induce a dizziness of the absolute, the productive vertigo that takes both readers and writer away from the belief in their individual selves so that they may realize how they are contingent and only fleetingly identical to their own names. *Museum of the Novel of the Eternal* was itself paralyzed in its creative possibilities by its will to be a manifesto. Its energy returns channeled through works by others, who wrote perhaps with less urgency than Macedonio, with less sense of a metaphysical mission, and with greater allegiance to the realm that is conventionally termed "literature." Macedonio's purist stand and high hopes for literature granted his text the role reserved for metaphysics and religion. In the process, Macedonio pointed out the staleness in those discourses, made them lighter, and gave to his writing the freshness of discovery and surprise. His literature required a reader who believed in his antinomies: realism and antirealism, Adriana and the "Eternal." Today, "el lector salteado"—the Skipping Reader—faithful to Macedonio's own sense of the liberating role of humor, skips over the distinction between one kind of representation and the other and, the lesson already assimilated, reads works celebrating the contamination and blurring of the "good" and "bad."

Notes

1. *Adriana Buenos Aires: The Last Bad Novel* appeared posthumously, in 1974. The pagination quoted in this chapter is cited according to Macedonio Fernández, *Adriana Buenos Aires; Ultima novela mala.* (Buenos Aires: Editorial Corregidor, 1974). The translations are my own. Jo Anne Engelbert observes that *Adriana* "not only failed to be the last bad novel, it even failed to be bad. Macedonio's frothing soap is one of his most appealing books." See Macedonio Fernández, *Macedonio: Selected Writings in Translation,* ed. Jo Anne Engelbert (Fort Worth, TX: Latitudes Press, 1984).

2. Adolfo de Obieta, Macedonio's son, is a rich source of biographical and bibliographical information about his father. In the 1974 edition of *Adriana Buenos Aires* he refers to Macedonio's perhaps serious, perhaps humorous plans for the Argentine presidency. For more on this issue see Dardo Cúneo, *El romanticismo político: Leopoldo Lugones, Roberto J. Payró, José Ingenieros, Macedonio Fernández, Manuel Ugarte, Alberto Gerchunoff* (Buenos Aires: Editorial Transición, 1955).

3. When I quote from *Museum of the Novel of the Eternal* the pagination corresponds to Macedonio Fernández, *Museo de la novela de la Eterna: Primera novela buena* (Buenos Aires: Centro Editor de América Latina, 1967); the translations are mine. I have studied this novel closely in my book *Macedonio Fernández y la teoría crítica: Una evaluación* (Buenos Aires: Editorial Corregidor, 1987). *MNE* is currently available in Editorial Corregidor (Buenos Aires, 1975).

4. Adolfo de Obieta recovers this dedication and the response in a footnote to his foreword in *Adriana Buenos Aires* (1974), p. 8. Alberto Hidalgo was a poet and close friend of Macedonio's. The position that Macedonio himself took regarding poetry was extremely disparaging. He had contempt for what he believed was a genre lacking in intelligence and dominated by "musiquitas"—trivial bits of music. He was reluctant to publish his own poetry, which appeared posthumously in Mexico. (See Macedonio Fernández, *Poemas* [Mexico City: Editorial Guarania, 1953]). Alberto Hidalgo, Macedonio Fernández, Vicente Huidobro, and Jorge Luis Borges wrote the prologue to a 1926 anthology of working poets, in which the view of poetry is less than flattering. See *Indice de la nueva poesía americana* (México and Buenos Aires: Sociedad de Publicaciones El Inca, 1926).

5. The world in which Macedonio lived was one of active literary conversation. Some of the literary magazines of the period tried to convey the rhythm of live discussion to their readership; such is the effect in *Revista Martín Fierro, Proa,* and *Nosotros,* on which Macedonio collaborated. The quotation of opinions by literary friends reproduces the kind of atmosphere prevalent in those literary journals.

6. "Para una teoría de la Humorística," in Macedonio Fernández, *Papeles de Recienvenido y continuación de la nada,* prologue by Ramón Gómez de la Serna (Buenos Aires: Losada, 1944; Centro Editor de América Latina, 1966; Editorial Corregidor, 1989). The translation of the title is mine.

7. Naomi Lindstrom offers an intelligent account of the polemical energy behind Macedonio's efforts in her *Macedonio Fernández* (Lincoln, NB: Society of Spanish and Spanish-American Studies, 1981). See also Germán Leopoldo García, ed., *Jorge Luis Borges, Arturo Jauretche y otros hablan de Macedonio Fernández* (Buenos Aires: Carlos Pérez Editor, 1969).

8. Vicente Huidobro and Macedonio Fernández shared the contempt they felt for mimetic literature and art; they parted ways, though, when it came time to decide which genre would be the best for practicing the new art. For Huidobro it was the poetic image, for Macedonio the new novel. See Vicente Huidobro, "Manifestos," in *Obras completas,* vol. 1 (Santiago: Editorial Zig Zag, 1976).

9. Jorge Luis Borges, "Diálogo sobre un diálogo," in *El Hacedor* (Buenos Aires: Emecé, 1961), p. 13.

10. Macedonio Fernández, *No toda es vigilia la de los ojos abiertos y otros escritos metafísicos* (Buenos Aires: Editorial Corregidor, 1967, 1990). An approximate translation of the awkward Spanish title is *Not All Is Open-Eyed Wakefulness and Other Metaphysical Writings.* This work is a metaphysical study in which Macedonio is at his most philosophical. He greatly admired William James and there are suggestions that they may have corresponded. As I researched the letters that I assembled in the volume of Macedonio's correspondence, however, I did not find any traces of such an exchange. It is possible, though, that letters were lost, given the many times Macedonio moved. See Macedonio Fernández, *Epistolario* (Buenos Aires: Editorial Corregidor, 1991).

11. See *Papeles de recienvenido* (1974). This book is conceived as a miscellany; it clearly demonstrates the diversity of Macedonio's interests and the range of his writing.

12. Julio Cortázar, *La vuelta al día en ochenta mundos* (México: Siglo XXI, 1967).

13. I study Morelli's view in Chapter 4 herein, devoted to Cortázar.

14. See Macedonio's *Epistolario.* Macedonio referred there to Ramón Gómez de la Serna as a "genio y esperanza de genio"—genius and hope of further genius. Their letters clearly express the sense of a common literary mission that united them.

15. Macedonio Fernández, *Museo de la Novela de la Eterna,* p. 66.

16. Leopoldo Marechal, *Adán Buenosayres* (Buenos Aires: Editorial Sudamericana, 1966).

Chapter 2
Taming the Reader: Jorge Luis Borges

> It is the animal with the big tail, a tail many yards long and like a fox's brush. How should I like to get my hands on this tail some time, but it is impossible, the animal is constantly moving about, the tail is constantly being flung this way and that. The animal resembles a kangaroo, but not as to the face, which is flat almost like a human face, and small and oval; only its teeth have power of expression, whether they are concealed or bared. Sometimes I have the feeling that the animal is trying to tame me. What other purpose could it have in withdrawing its tail when I snatch at it, and then again, waiting calmly until I am tempted again, and then leaping away once more?
> —Franz Kafka, "Dearest Father"[1]

Who is in Charge?

The "animal imagined by Kafka," revived by Borges in *The Book of Imaginary Beings,* holds a powerful grip on Borges and the reader. It is the ultimate source of confusion, which is found time and again in legend and myth: it partakes of human traits but is not human, its strength is derived from the familiarity of a first look at its face and its threatening animal-like features. The thought of domestication implies that there is something wild there, something to be subsumed by the human stare, in an unstable relationship prone to sudden reversals, since *it* could try to tame *us*. In Kafka the *I* in danger of being overtaken by a logic that it does not quite understand is always slipping into an *us* that engulfs the reader, turning him or her into the protagonist of a boundary crossing.

Borges has stated his interest in Kafka more than once. The turns that upset established relationships, such as the friendship between Don Quixote and Sancho as depicted by Kafka,[2] are revealing of the ways in which Borges himself views issues of control and authorship.

The animal imagined by Kafka is an orphan, indicating no concern with origins. A mixed breed par excellence, this creature questions our own origins as we observe the combination of its features. Do works of literature and art disconcert us in the same way? Are we disturbed if we do not perceive their unity, their *coherence*? The search for literary attributions is an expression of enthusiasm for the integration of works into the kind of sequential historical narrative that gives a meaning to what otherwise might appear to be disjointed, endowed with the uncanniness of the animal evoked by Kafka. For Borges written works are objects such as that animal. They threaten to domesticate us through the power of their peculiar secrets. In the Kafka evocation, the bond between us and the animal is made of stares: it looks at us and we look at it without being able to state who understands whom, and it is, therefore, able to prevail in an exercise in which knowledge amounts to authority.

In Kafka we read about the intricate ways in which we end up relinquishing our will to understand as we submit to a logic we cannot grasp; Borges's fascination with Kafka points to the intense affinity of their efforts. Privileged objects such as Borges's aleph and zahir[3] fix the attention and aspirations of characters who submit to them without completely knowing what they are. But it is in our relationship to reading that the battle for control takes place in ways that are—for Borges—filled with the kind of danger and suspense to be found in tales of adventure.

One of the most gripping of such tales is "The Book of Sand,"[4] in which a man acquires a peculiar book from a traveling salesman. Described as a sacred and infinite volume, this book soon occupies all its owner's time. As he turns the pages, their order and numbering make it impossible to read them in a sequential order. The writing, moreover, is in characters he does not understand. The solution appears to him with utmost clarity: he must get rid of this book, which he perceives as both monstrous and obscene, for, in a Kafkian turn, he feels that he is himself becoming an obscene monster merely by turning its pages. After abandoning the idea of burning it, because the fire elicited by an infinite book might destroy the universe, he decides to lose it by leaving it on a shelf in a Buenos Aires library.

The threat has now been generalized. The man may very well be free from the spell of the book, but what about us? What awaits us on a library shelf? How do we know that we will not encounter the danger of the all-engrossing and yet incomprehensible and infinite book that might swallow up, as we try to understand it, every other ambition and interest we may entertain? The perils presented in "The Book of Sand" are radical; it is the self that is at stake in the unstability of the reading provoked by an utterly foreign volume. The happy ending of the story saves the main character by allowing him to lose the book instead of losing himself. The converse of that ending is that the threat is now directed toward the reader, thereby suggesting the need for a suspicious relationship to libraries.

"The Book of Sand" answers quite clearly the question of who is in charge: it is the book, and its power resides precisely in the secrecy of its words and format. But whereas here the reader has been thoroughly "tamed," in Kafka's sense, by the triumphing book, "Pierre Menard, Author of *Don Quixote*"[5] tries to tell an opposite story.

Who Owns an Author's Style?

In contrast to "The Book of Sand," which remains almost a hypothesis, Cervantes's *Don Quixote* is a widely known work, written, moreover, in Borges's own Spanish. *Don Quixote* has also been thoroughly studied and, we might say, "tamed," by abundant literary commentary. Its status as a classic of Western culture endows it with a grounding rather than a destabilizing force, part of a reassuring shared culture despite its being removed in time from our present experience.

"Pierre Menard, Author of *Don Quixote*," written from the point of view of a reviewer with mixed feelings about his subject matter, presents Pierre Menard, who wants to rewrite *Don Quixote*.

The initial method he conceived was relatively simple: to know Spanish well, to re-embrace the Catholic faith, to fight against Moors and Turks, to forget European history between 1602 and 1918 and to be Miguel de Cervantes. Pierre Menard studied this procedure (I know that he arrived at a rather faithful handling of seventeenth-century Spanish) but rejected it as too easy. Rather because it was impossible, the reader will say! (p. 49)

The reviewer, a friend of Menard's, wants to secure his own complicity with the reader by inserting criticisms and pieces of information about his subject designed to elicit a humorously critical reaction from the public.

Menard is trying to gain access to *Don Quixote* by reproducing it; as in numerous other instances in Borges's work we find here a parody of the excesses of the kind of literature and literary criticism bound by an uncompromising faithfulness to a remote original.[6] But Menard's project does not consist of mere mimicry, however difficult it might be. The way in which he approaches his task betrays an acute awareness of the passage of time; he rejects total identification with Cervantes in favor of a dual embodiment, for we are told that he decides to be both Pierre Menard and Miguel de Cervantes.

What kind of identity is preserved by Menard in contrast to the one he has as Cervantes? Menard is a French symbolist from Nîmes who expresses a certain disdain for *Don Quixote* and considers it an "accidental book."[7]

> "*Don Quixote*," Menard explains, "interests me profoundly, but it does not seem to have been—how shall I say it—inevitable. I cannot imagine the universe without the interjection of Edgar Allan Poe 'Ah, bear in mind this garden was enchanted!' or without the 'Bateau ivre' or the 'Ancient Mariner,' but I know that I am capable of imagining it without *Don Quixote*. (I speak, naturally, of my personal capacity, not of the historical repercussions of these works.) *Don Quixote* is an accidental book, *Don Quixote* is unnecessary. I can premeditate writing it, I can write it without incurring a tautology." (p. 50)

Menard is a writer who, in undertaking the difficult task of becoming another, expresses contempt for his own project. *Don Quixote* barely interests him; he even volunteers that "My general memory of *Don Quixote*, simplified by forgetfulness and indifference, is much the same as the imprecise, anterior image of a book not yet written" (p. 51).

Menard's main category of self-definition is time; he can only remain separate from Cervantes if he defines the excellence of his own production of *Don Quixote* by the historical distance that separates him from Cervantes. Menard asks to be rewarded because of the effort involved in overcoming his double foreignness—his native language is French, not Spanish, and he is writing in the twentieth century. But how is it possible for him to preserve anything of himself while writing Cervantes's words and, as he says, "becoming Cervantes"? His own identity and authorship are attested to by a group of friends and reviewers who, representing his own community of interpretation, praise or denigrate his work, which shows us the literary environment from which he emerges. Thus Menard has been able to forge for himself a double persona, distinct from and yet identical to Cervantes.

The reviewer gives an example of Menard's art as a way of showing us the extent to which he achieved the aims of his project. The excerpt is a well-known passage from *Don Quixote*: "truth, whose mother is history, who is the rival of time, depository of deeds, witness of the past, example and lesson to the present, and warning to the future" (p. 51). We realize that this fragment is the very moment in *Don Quixote* in which its authorship is questioned, because the suspicion has been raised that the preceding part of the novel may be a translation of a work of unknown origin produced by unreliable sources. In this way, Menard's sense of himself as being different from Cervantes is perceived as an illusion, because he has reproduced exactly, although unknowingly, the situation in *Don Quixote* portraying Cervantes as the contested author of an original redefined as a dubious translated version.[8]

"Pierre Menard, Author of *Don Quixote*" presents a gallery of characters who are to be laughed at because of their snobbishness or their mistaken tastes for literary experimentation, including the narrator himself, a reviewer with a limited capacity for friendship and a petty need for recognition. Pierre Menard is, of course, laughable as well, insofar as he represents an extreme of abstruse literary experimentation. But beyond the comic overtones, his attempts stand for the impossibility of keeping the kind of reassuring distance that preserves the self.

Menard wanted to be a sort of literary tourist, with a round-trip ticket to *Don Quixote* that would return him to his own identity; instead, he was appropriated by the words he was trying to make his own. In reproducing the section from *Don Quixote,* he merged his identity with that of Cervantes, but the pleasure of disrupting tradition was denied him; the tourist was denied the uniqueness of his voyage because Cervantes himself became part of the imitative chain.

Menard and Cervantes belong to the same mimetic series; they may be distinguished from each other, we are told, by their *style*. Through the use of the same words each of them has practiced a different style; Menard had hoped that as a consequence he would be able to use those words for his own purposes. Instead, like Cervantes, he became part of the secondariness already present in the "original" work. A member of the Menard literary circle, the narrator-reviewer who supplies the background information, frames the story by alerting us to its implicit ideal addressee:

> Menard (perhaps without wishing to) has enriched, by means of a new technique, the hesitant and rudimentary art of reading: the technique is one of deliberate anachronism and erroneous attributions. This technique, with its infinite applications, urges us to run through the *Odyssey* as if it were written after the *Aeneid,* and to read *Le jardin du centaur* by Madame Henri Bachelier as if it were written by Madame Henri Bachelier. This technique would fill the dullest books with adventure. Would not the attributing of the *Imitation of Christ* to Louis-Ferdinand Céline or James Joyce be a sufficient renovation of its tenuous spiritual counsels? (pp. 54–55)

Thus the reviewer suggests that Menard's experiment is, indeed, a renewal of our literary view. It offers the notion of authorship as a shift in the question of perspective and institutes the possibility of a level of irony that redefines the contents of what we are reading. But we must also consider our own attitude regarding the reviewer. In understanding what we are reading in terms of style we have also become acutely aware of the reviewer's faults. His statements are suspect because they emerge from a maze of personal mannerisms. If we are to be faithful to Menard's general project as an emphasis of the notion of style that, in his case, means tone and point of view, we must reflect on the credibility of the reviewer. The text, signed in 1939 in Nîmes, offers this commentary:

> It is, therefore, impossible to forgive the omissions and additions perpetrated by Madame Henri Bachelier in a fallacious catalogue that a certain newspaper, whose Protestant tendencies are no secret, was inconsiderate enough to inflict on its wretched readers—even though they are few and Calvinist, if not Masonic and circumcised. (p. 45)

The identification of the reviewer with the ideological and religious intolerance of 1939 France is clear. The choice of such a context for the presentation and praise of Menard's project is of great importance because we are given the clues to infer that Menard, as a member of the same community, shares these beliefs or is at least in a situation where those concerns are permanently present.

Thus the reviewer's style, exclusionary of some and suggestive of intimacy with others, forces us to take a position about Menard's project even before we know about its particularities and intricacies. The highlighting of the historical and social context conveys its own set of messages to the reader, forging a complementary narrative. This complementary fiction retells the story of the part of *Don Quixote* reproduced by Menard by emphasizing its dismissal of Moors and gypsies as agents of lies, while casting the sympathies of both Menard and the reviewer in the success of those exclusionary efforts. Mentions of Maurice Barrès, Louis-Ferdinand Céline, and Léon Daudet lend even more intensity to this vision, whereas the association with Enrique Rodríguez Larreta (called rather cruelly *Dr.* Rodríguez Larreta)[9] adds a comical note to the idea of national purity.

The reviewer supports national purity of several sorts, which is one of the sources of humor in this piece, elicited, for example, by the mention of one of Menard's works, a translation into French of Francisco Gómez de Quevedo's indictment of Luis de Góngora, "Aguja de navegar cultos," "La boussole des precieux."[10] Menard extols national purity so much that he wants to have a taste of two pure national cultures: early twentieth-century France and seventeenth-century Spain.

Is the story telling us that Cervantes and Menard can indeed have a common project because they belong to equally exclusionary historical times? Is the paragraph reproduced by Menard of such a force that it equals the feelings that French fascists might have felt if they had lived at that time?

Although we are not presented with answers to these questions, the fact that they can be posed allows for some reflections regarding the meaning of rewriting elicited by the story. "Pierre Menard, Author of *Don Quixote*" offers a project of rewriting in which literary repetition is also found in history so that the writer cannot preserve his own identity or, conversely, efface it to become someone else he has chosen to be. The energy of both history and literature is such that writer—or rewriter—cannot be a tourist; he cannot go back home. Menard, like Cervantes, is forced by "truth, whose mother is history, who is the rival of time, depository of deeds, witness of the past, example and lesson to the present, and warning to the future," to rehearse once and again words that precipitate wars, friendships, a sense of beauty. Menard is not any freer than Cervantes in choosing the effect of his writing or rewriting as style. An ideal implicit and complicitous reader is necessary to assess the meaning of their story and to redefine it through laughter or the seriousness of an uncompromising stare.

The preservation and careful meditation about distance found throughout Borges's work is rendered here, again, as an impossibility whose very cracks constitute what we interpret to be our freedom, or, in "Menardian" terms, our style.

The Paradoxes of Belonging: Jews and History

Pierre Menard remains an element in a construct that repeats history through a continuous restaging of exclusionary politics. Zimerman, a character in Borges's story "Guayaquil,"[11] attempts not to rewrite a text but to interpret it and, in the course of the exercise, is thrust—like Menard—into history.

The story is told by a pompous and melancholy narrator who introduces himself as a member of patrician Argentine stock. His main credentials are represented by his family roots in Argentine history. The house he lives in has belonged to his family for generations, his ancestors fought in pertinent wars; in short, he is the latest offspring in an undisturbed chain of "pure" Argentines. He also holds a membership in the Argentine National Historical Academy. The story he tells us concerns the visit of a foreign-born Jewish historian, Zimerman, to whom he reacts in disgust, making no secret of his antisemitic feelings. The reason for the visit concerns a historical document on which both men are interested in working. It is a letter by Simón Bolívar from Cartagena, dated August 13, 1824, in which he gives details of his encounter with José de San Martín in Guayaquil. The interest of the document is, of course, that it is presented as though it could shed light onto that meeting, so shrouded in historical mystery, when San Martín gave up the glories of the campaigns of Latin American liberation to Bolívar.

The narrator describes with revelatory disapproval some of Zimerman's traits: his head is too big, his mispronunciation of Spanish abounds with German inflections, his suit is not elegant, his face is too complicated, his manner is too polite for comfort. There is no doubt that in the framework of this story, the narrator feels that he *belongs* where he is; he has been prepared by generations to occupy his place in history, whereas Zimerman, merely a newcomer, is a disagreeable intruder.

Zimerman, aware of the difference in their origins, expresses his own right to decipher the document in the following manner:

—"In the blood. You are the genuine historian. Your people lived in the vast lands of America and fought its great battles, while mine, somberly, was barely emerging from the ghetto. You carry history in your blood, according to your own eloquent words; for you it is enough to listen to that ancestral voice. In my case, instead, I must go to Sulaco and decipher paper after paper of perhaps apocryphal origins. Believe me, doctor, I envy you. (p. 1065)

Aside from Zimerman's possible mockery of the roots that make his host a historian "in the blood," there is an important displacement: reading and interpreting documents is not seen as a right given by a shared heritage but as a somewhat tedious occupation to be held by wanderers. The meeting between San Martín and Bolívar has ceased to be an event affecting primarily those who feel themselves to be direct descendents of their struggles; it has become the stuff of possible apocryphal versions, a dark knot to be made tighter by further rewritings and rereadings.

The narrator wants the complicity of the readers and asks them to share his contempt for Zimerman's ways and his faulty Spanish; Zimerman tells him, implicitly, that because he is too perfectly settled in his patrician world and his Spanish is too perfect, the realm of historical interpretation he has chosen as a profession may elude him. Viewed in this manner, "Guayaquil" describes an impossible landscape, an endlessly questionable source for the production of documents. The Argentine historian relinquishes the right to interpret the document to Zimerman in a gesture that superimposes their encounter on the one between San Martín and Bolívar. Thus the interpretation of history is to be left to an outsider and denied to those with familial ties. Zimerman, cast in the role of intruder by the narrator's antisemitism, is also the one who holds the key to the mystery of the encounter between San Martín and Bolívar.

Why did the patrician Argentine historian give Zimerman that advantage? Was it merely to let him play with documents of a history that he could interpret but never own? Or was it because they were fated—by the nature of the enigma of what occurred in Guayaquil—to reenact the scene played out there, where one man gave up his privilege to another, leaving the explanation to interpreters of various sorts? If this second alternative is the answer, Zimerman would have found his place in history precisely because of the Argentine historian's need to acquiesce to a logic that had prepared him for generations to do precisely what San Martín did: give up Guayaquil.

Unknowingly, just as Pierre Menard became entangled in the "original" situation of the text of *Don Quixote* that he produced, the two historians, one an intruder and the other native born, have produced the best interpretation either one of them has seen, through its reenactment. Being Jewish becomes a category for this sort of exchange; Zimerman represents a loss of place and roots, and his reward is a privileged mobility, a capacity for access to the *words* of history if not participation in its events. But as he is also, like Menard, tamed by the event he wants to interpret, we are led to wonder about who might have been in the position of Zimerman in the original scene at Guayaquil. History, as it is repeated, is not explained away. On the contrary, it is here constituted as a puzzling question asked through different voices with similar urgency.

Answers

As characters wander in Borges's stories through gardens and libraries, rethinking sometimes with humor and often with profound sadness issues of repetition, eternity, and racial animosity,[12] some of them come up with answers to their quests. Their results do not always send them back to puzzling situations that offer neither shelter nor reassurance; one such instance is found in "The Aleph."[13]

Two characters, one named Borges and the other Carlos Argentino, are linked by a rivalry for Beatriz Viterbo, a woman who died. Theirs is a rather petty friendship; the love for Beatriz does not obscure her defects—on the contrary it serves to suggest one of Borges's recurring insights: that love for a woman is often illuminating of the enamored's lapses in taste. Carlos Argentino's goal is to write a poem that summarizes the universe; he does, in fact, produce some stanzas shown to be ridiculous for their pompousness.

Borges, telling the story in his own name, conveys the boredom and condescension he feels when he is with Carlos Argentino. And yet his own find in the story is an object, called an *aleph,* which contains the whole universe. As he looks at it in the basement of a house about to be demolished, he is able to see his own past, very distant lands and times simultaneously, and confronts the issue of how to convey what he has seen to others. Communicating his discovery soon becomes out of the question because he realizes that he could do so only in a language that is successive in nature, which would be counter to his experience of simultaneous perception. Carlos Argentino, from upstairs, calls to him and urges him, mockingly, to describe the object, which he judges to be nonexistent. Borges opts for lying, denying the aleph's existence and finally forgetting that he has seen it:

> "You saw it all, in colors?"
> It was at that instant that I conceived my revenge. Benevolently, with obvious pity, nervous, evasive, I thanked Carlos Argentino for the hospitality of his cellar and urged him to take advantage of the demolition of his house to get far away from the pernicious capital, which is easy on no one, believe me, on no one! I refused with suave energy, to discuss the Aleph; I embraced him on leaving, and repeated that the country and its quiet are two grand doctors.
> In the street, on the Constitución stairs, in the subway, all the faces struck me as familiar. I feared that not a single thing was to cause me surprise; I was afraid I would never be quit of the impression that I had "returned." Happily, at the end of a few nights of insomnia, forgetfulness took hold of me again. (p. 152)[14]

The Aleph, then, exists. It serves to grant a position of privilege to Borges, who keeps it as his own secret, and to debase Carlos Argentino, whose own literary project wants nothing else but to produce its literary equivalent. Like the book of sand, this infinite object may be lost, but unlike the book, the Aleph does not hold Borges hostage to its simultaneity; it accompanies him as a secret and a suppressed memory. Through it, Borges acquires a prestige that differentiates him from Carlos Argentino. The difference lies in the fact that Carlos Argentino evokes, in a faulty language, a universe that he knows only partially, whereas Borges has opted for silence. The aristocratic solution of how to deal with this sort of object, which is simultaneously an answer to a quest for Borges, is silence.

Such is the lesson to be derived from another of Borges's exemplary tales, "The Writing of the God."[15] There a man condemned to prison is contemplating a tiger, pacing in another cell, next to his own. When he ponders his situation, he realizes that the key to mysteries he had tried to unravel throughout his life is to be derived from the spots of the tiger, but this understanding cannot be transmitted to anybody else. Like the silent tiger, the man has reached a level of awareness beyond spoken language.

The hypothesis that there is something sacred, because of its beauty, wisdom, or terror, that remains unspeakable permeates Borges's works. That "something" grounds quests and constitutes the ultimate aim of many of his characters.

If a reading of Borges's fiction is often framed by considerations of humor and an understanding of layers that relativize what is being said, his poetry tends to be more straightforward in the statement of his intentions.

Borges approached poetry with caution, concerned (like Macedonio Fernández) with the risk of emotional excesses.[16] From the 1920s, when his first volumes of poetry appeared, he speaks of his intense roots in Buenos Aires, his favorite books, and occasionally love—subjects he would not abandon during his long career. It is to be expected, then, that a key may be found in his poetry, where the unspeakable is rendered with eloquence.

"The Other Tiger"[17] attempts to render its image in an autobiographical tone:

> I think of a tiger. The gloom here makes
> The vast and busy Library seem lofty
> And pushes the shelves back;
> Strong, innocent, covered with blood and new,
> It will move through its forest and its morning . . . (p. 70)

The poem suggests that the awareness of the tiger's body, of the tiger *as body* is strong; not only is it "covered with blood and new" but it

> will print its tracks on the muddy
> Margins of a river whose name it does not know."

The poet thinks of this tiger, as in "The Writing of the God," as a writing pad with a carnality left intact by its availability to decoding:

> Between the stripes of the bamboo I decipher
> Its stripes and have the feel of the bony structure
> That quivers under the glowing skin.

The realization that this tiger

> Is a ghost of a tiger, a symbol
> A series of literary tropes
> And memories from the encyclopaedia
> And not the deadly tiger, the fateful jewel

makes the poet aware of the limitations of writing. The poem does not posit, however, a mere opposition between imagination and the real, since it recognizes the function that naming performs in conferring linguistic status on everything:

> . . . conjecturing its circumstance
> Makes it a figment of art and no creature
> Living among those that walk the earth.

Nor is Borges interested in celebrating the dismantling of the real or truth by language; he is not a complacent deconstructor. The poem ends with an invitation to search for still another tiger.

> We shall seek a third tiger. This
> Will be like those others a shape
> Of my dreaming, a system of words
> A man makes and not the vertebrate tiger
> That, beyond the mythologies
> Is treading the earth. I know well enough
> That something lays on me this quest
> Undefined, senseless and ancient, and I go on
> Seeking through the afternoon time
> That other tiger, that which is not in verse. (p. 71)

"That other tiger, that which is not in verse" provides the formulation for the ultimate resolution in Borges's work; it gives its charge to language while still escaping it, prompting us to go further. Borges's fascination with the scene evoked by Kafka's animal describes the fear and inevitability involved in our relationship to that which impels us to know more, to think again. Silence and the conciliation of oppositions, animated by a reverence for what lies behind and a thrust toward transcendence, are favorite endings for Borges.

Although Borges's writing points toward the metaphysical, toward the ways in which language meanders in the direction of the ungraspable, his sense of that realm is profoundly cultural. Familiarity with his work leads to a notion of reading as rewriting, of an active involvement in an exercise that could plunge us into the tabula rasa of the empiricists, Jewish mysticism, rabbinics, historical repetitions à la Zimerman and Menard, and the loss of self in "The Book of Sand."

A conversation with Borges about literature never felt as though one had chosen a particular subject among others. In his slow, deliberate voice he managed to convey that this was the only topic worth discussing, precisely because he could turn it into an aleph, the privileged object of a quest, the valued secret of those in the know, the recovered memory of a wisdom once held. The complicities elicited by literature interested him intensely, as he researched and wrote stories about sects, cenacles, and tribes. His own gift for intimacy resided precisely in his capacity to converse by creating a bond with his interlocutor through literature.

Borges has been portrayed as the supreme intellectual author, one who would always make sure that the priority was on the side of books. It is important to note that for him it was not a matter of choice. If literature was in charge it was because he thought, and felt, that life was charged by it and did not exist in the opposition so touted by both facile materialists and idealists. An aversion for long-winded phrases and novels animates Borges's capacity for synthesis, so that readers remain in touch, throughout his work, with a sense of both urgency and respect for the brevity of the relationship between themselves and the page.

Was Borges interested in building a theory of literature? He certainly spoke and wrote with admiration about his friend and predecessor, Macedonio Fernández, who says in his *Museum of the Novel of the Eternal*[18] that he is not sure whether he has written a novel or a theory of the novel. Unlike Macedonio Fernández, though, Borges was not bound by the limitations that a protracted, coherent, theoretical language implies. He was indeed inclined to take his texts to their ultimate conclusions and make them spin against their own certainties, but the quality that dominates his writing is the sense that theory may be the best of fictions.

When we laugh at Pierre Menard and the other fictional authors who populate Borges's works, as well as those written in collaboration with Adolfo Bioy Casares,[19] we sense the distance that Borges placed himself at from a certain earnestness in literature, and the antipathy he had for the theoretical as exclusionary. Pierre Menard is, among other things, somewhat crazy; his madness entails taking his own attempts too seriously, being too coherent, an aspect that brings him close to Don Quixote. Zimerman wins the battle for the Guayaquil document because he is able to use to his advantage the dogmatic vision of the relationship between history and the personal roots of his nationalistic competitor. The character—Borges—who seizes and sees the aleph can do so because he understands Carlos Argentino's ridiculing the belief in such objects.

Borges's interests, then, are indeed theoretical. His answers, however, do not privilege one theoretical view; on the contrary, they posit the quest for the ungraspable realm as that which, in charging literature with meaning, becomes accessible by humor and proliferation.

A Twist

Literature in Borges is the source of mangled messages, of texts as plural and disquieting as a Kafkian mixed-breed creature. Sometimes, however, a swift, univocal resolution to a story allows a glimpse from a different angle of his sense of what matters.

"The Intruder"[20] offers a version of a love triangle. Two men living in the same house in a rural town see their closeness threatened by the presence of a woman whose sexual favors they both covet. A rivalry develops between them. She is described as being untalkative and rather vulgar in appearance. After one of the men sells her to a brothel, they discover that both of them go there to obtain her favors. The relationship between the men has been altered by this woman, who interferes with their fellowship and precipitates unloyal behavior. From the perspective of the story, the male bond that preserves the harmony of their world has been broken by a contingency, their shared desire for a woman. The brutal ending of the tale is a happy one, within its misogynistic point of view: one of the men takes charge and kills the intruder. We learn of the murder when the killer tells the other man that everything is over, they can both go back to their work and let her be finished off by birds of prey.

The logic of this love triangle favors male friendship and the courage necessary to preserve that bond. The story abounds in indications that this circumstance is a recasting of old situations; its novelty resides in the clarity with which the two do away with the intruder and the lack of room for reinterpretation, since there is no basis in the story for the reader's solidarity with any characters except the male friends.

Having reconciled, the two men leave us with the difficult legacy of their faithfulness to each other. Another murder arising from faithfulness appears in the "Scripture According to Mark,"[21] in which a condescending and nonbelieving character from the city arrives in a rural town, where he reads the Gospel according to Mark to a group of peasants who end up crucifying him as he comes to the episode of the crucifixion. The crucifixion is a humorous take on the possibility of a literal interpretation, and the condemnation of the nonbeliever by its force constitutes a sinister acknowledgment of the peasants' attitude about the scriptures.

Knifings and murders appear frequently in Borges's writing. He admired the way in which such deaths define the shape of individual destiny, their status as an ultimate medium for consecrating the inevitability of plots beyond the grasp of those enmeshed in them. Physical violence is rarely expressed in his words, however, for it is not the physiological aspect of death—the specific circumstances of blood and the infliction of pain—that interests him; it is, rather, a poetics of completion. The decisive points in Borges's emotional landscape—Buenos Aires, tango, and libraries—are reshuffled time and again in his work, but only sudden death by murder has the power of framing life by its termination. Borges tried to invent endings for his characters that would assure their role in an ideal plot, beyond their control.

If Borges's fables about writing and history take us to the realm of the transcendent through repetition, his apparently "realistic" stories are a way of denying the shapelessness of life, the hypothesis of a longevity without purpose. For whatever reasons, Borges was granted long life; how we might intuit the ultimate shape of the plot that led him to die in Geneva rather than in Buenos Aires, the city that most intensely animated his writing, remains our intimate challenge.

Notes

1. From Franz Kafka, "Dearest Father" (1919) (translated from the German by Ernst Kaiser and Eithne Wilkins), as quoted by Jorge Luis Borges in his *Book of Imaginary Beings*, trans. Norman Thomas di Giovanni (New York: E. P. Dutton, 1970), p. 26.
2. See, for example, Jorge Luis Borges, "Kafka y sus precursores," in *Obras completas* (Buenos Aires: Emecé, 1974), p. 710, as well as, in the same volume "Magias parciales del Quijote," p. 667.
3. "El Aleph" and "El Zahir" originally appeared in 1949 as part of a collection of stories under the title of *El Aleph*. Sylvia Molloy studies the role played by what she calls "las metáforas desglosadas" (in Borges's writing), pointing out their role in keeping the uncanniness of the text intact; privileged objects such as the zahir and the aleph perform the same function. See Sylvia Molloy, "Inquietud y conversion del simulacro," *Las letras de Borges* (Buenos Aires: Editorial Sudamericana, 1979), pp. 138–61.
4. Jorge Luis Borges, "The Book of Sand," in *Obras completas*, vol. 2, pp. 11–72.
5. The pagination corresponds to Jorge Luis Borges, "Pierre Menard, Author of *Don Quixote*," in *Ficciones* (New York: Grove Press, 1962). Emir Rodríguez Monegal suggests the intricacies of Borges's relationship to French culture through a study of some of the references behind the choice of Menard's name in this story: "A footnote to Louis Menard. In De Gourmont's article, in talking about the invention of collodium, the author indicates that an American inventor 'rediscovered' collodium and took the precaution of taking out an international patent under his own name which was (confusion compounded) Maynard: a name that in French sounds almost the same as Menard. The whole story is already too Borgesian." See Emir Rodríguez Monegal, *Jorge Luis Borges: A Literary Biography* (New York: E. P. Dutton, 1978), p. 123. For a study of the consequences elicited by Menard's art of superimposition, see Jeffrey Mehlman's "Pierre Menard, Author of *Don Quixote* Again," *L'esprit créateur* 22, 4 (Winter 1983): 22–37.
6. John Sturrock remarks: "From the reader's point of view there can be no ideal coincidence between Menard's chapters of *Don Quijote* and the original.

Indeed, from the reader's point of view there have never been two identical texts of any book because no book has ever been read with identical responses by two people, nor by the same person twice." See John Sturrock, "Odium Theologicum," in Harold Bloom, ed., *Jorge Luis Borges* (New York: Chelsea House, 1986), p. 161.

7. The parody of French culture present in "Pierre Menard, Author of *Don Quixote*" is a testimony to the complicated relationship Borges had to France. Emir Rodríguez Monegal in his literary biography of Borges maintains that he never quite abandoned the French despite the occasional signs he gave in that direction. See Rodríguez Monegal, *Jorge Luis Borges*. John Irwin holds the opposite opinion in "The Journey to the South: Poe, Borges and Faulkner," *Virginia Quarterly Review* 67, 3 (Summer 1991): 417–31.

8. Vladimir Nabokov reflects on the fragment of *Don Quixote* reproduced by Menard (without mentioning Borges) and considers the advantage of the hypothesis of a translation by a Moor: "Cervantes also protects himself, as later authors were to do, by appeals to the authority of the history that he had translated and to the fact that its Moorish author was a guarantee against hyperbole applied to a Spanish hero." See Vladimir Nabokov, *Lectures on Don Quixote* (New York: Harcourt Brace Jovanovich, 1983), p. 77. The issue at stake in Borges's recasting is an opposite attitude: historical accuracy is questioned from Cervantes to the present and hyperbole is regarded as an unfortunate component of literary production.

9. Rodríguez Larreta attempted seriously in his *La gloria de Don Ramiro* a kind of historical reconstruction that some—I include Borges here—saw as laughable because of its relentless solemnity.

10. Quevedo's attack on Góngora is an early occurrence of the strife toward purity evoked in this Borges text.

11. Jorge Luis Borges, "Guayaquil," in *El informe de Brodie* (Buenos Aires: Emecé, 1970). Page numbers correspond to this edition.

12. These issues are found throughout Borges's work. His *Historia del tango* provides an excellent example of how he views the interplay between regional and universal forms of expression. See *Historia del tango* in volume 1 of the 1989 edition of *Obras completas*. For a polemical view of Borges's stands, see Noé Jitrik, *Escritores argentinos: Dependencia o libertad* (Buenos Aires: Ediciones del Candil, 1967) as well as his "Estructura y significado en *Ficciones* de Jorge Luis Borges," included in the volume *Contra Borges* edited by Juan Fló (Buenos Aires: Galerna, 1978). The virulence of the charges against Borges's opinions regarding literature and national identity is now past, together with the specific political realities that precipitated the attacks. Regarding Borges's broader relationship to Latin American culture, see Julio Ortega, "Borges y la cultura hispanoamericana," *Revista Iberoamericana* 100–101 (1967): 257–68, as well as Saúl Yurkievich, *Fundadores de la nueva poesía latinoamericana* (Barcelona: Seix Barral, 1971). James Irby studies Borges's links with local references in "Borges, Carriego y el arrabal," in Jaime Alazraki, ed., *Jorge Luis Borges* (Madrid: Taurus, 1976), pp. 252–57.

13. Jorge Luis Borges, "El Aleph," in *El Aleph* (Buenos Aires: Emecé, 1962). Page numbers correspond to that edition. Walter Mignolo's study "Emergencia, espacio, 'Mundos posibles': las propuestas epistemologicas de Jorge Luis Borges," *Revista Iberoamericana* 100–101 (1967): 337–56, rehearses the scientism of arguments such as those found in "The Aleph." Borges's universalizing epistemological fictions had a great influence on what would become the

structuralist and poststructuralist view of literature and culture. See Michel Foucault, *Les mots et les choses: une archéologie des sciences humaines* (Paris: Gallimard, 1966), Gerard Genette, "L'utopie litteraire," in *Figures, essaìes* (Paris: Éditions du Seuil, 1966), and Emir Rodríguez Monegal, "Borges y la 'Nouvelle Critique,'" in Alazraki, *Jorge Luis Borges*, pp. 267–87.

14. My translation.

15. Jorge Luis Borges, "La escritura del dios," in *El Aleph*. Borges's interests in exploring religious and mystical avenues led him to approach various traditions; one of his most haunting pursuits remained that of the Kabala. See Saúl Sosnowski, *Borges y la Cábala: la búsqueda del verbo* (Buenos Aires: Hispamérica, 1976), and Ana María Barrenechea's *La expresión de la irrealidad en la obra de Jorge Luis Borges* (México: Colegio de México, 1957). Borges talked to Osvaldo Ferrari about his own position regarding the existence of an absolute being during the course of an interview published in a most engaging volume. See Osvaldo Ferrari and Jorge Luis Borges, "Borges descree de una divinidad personal," in *Diálogos últimos* (Barcelona: Seix Barral, 1992), pp. 63–67.

16. This may be the reason behind the use of English rather than Spanish in some of Borges's love poems.

17. See Jorge Luis Borges, "The Other Tiger," in *A Personal Anthology* (New York: Grove Press, 1967), pp. 81–82. Among the studies of Borges's poetry see Guillermo Sucre, *Borges, el poeta* (México: UNAM, 1967), and Yurkievich, *Fundadores de la neuva poesía latinoamericana*. Gerardo Mario Goloboff elaborates on the interconnections between the different genres practiced by Borges, paying special attention to his poetry and his concept of metaphor, in *Leer Borges* (Buenos Aires: Huemul, 1978).

18. See Chapter 1 in this volume.

19. See Jorge Luis Borges, *Obras completas en colaboración* (Buenos Aires: Emecé, 1979).

20. Jorge Luis Borges, "La intrusa," in *El informe de Brodie* (Buenos Aires: Emecé, 1970). Estela Canto's personal evocation of her romantic relationship with Borges contains a reading of "La intrusa" in which she casts herself as the intruder and suggests that Borges and his mother were in the position of the two males in the story. See Estela Canto, *Borges a contraluz* (Madrid: Espasa Calpe, 1989). One is tempted to recall in this regard Vladimir Nabokov's advice to a literary critic: "Learn to distinguish banality. Remember that mediocrity thrives on 'ideas.' Beware of the moddish message. Ask yourself if the symbol you have detected is not your own footprint." Vladimir Nabokov, *Strong Opinions* (New York: McGraw-Hill, 1973), p. 66.

21. Borges, "El Evangelio según Marcos," in *El informe de Brodie*. For a sampling of texts of particular interest to Borges and Bioy Casares on these issues, see their own anthology, Jorge Luis Borges and Adolfo Bioy Casares, *Libro del cielo y del infierno* (Barcelona: EDHASA, 1971), as well as Jorge Luis Borges, *Libro de sueños* (Buenos Aires: Torres Agüero Editor, 1976).

Chapter 3
Intelligence and Its Neighbors: Gabriel García Márquez

> The few women left in town, like Clotilde, were boiling up with bitterness. And like her, there was old Jacob's wife, who got up earlier than usual that morning, put the house in order, and sat down to breakfast with a look of adversity. "My last wish," she said to her husband, "is to be buried alive."
> —Gabriel García Márquez, "The Sea of Lost Time"[1]

Is There a Book in This Book?

Reading Borges leaves us with the need to look further in other books, visit libraries in pursuit of the adventure he maps out for us. García Márquez holds a very different kind of grip on his readers. His is a literature that attempts to draw us into a complete world, with its own cadences and rules. Jacob's wife, the woman in the epigraph who wishes above all to be buried alive, not only gives us a hyperbolic understanding of despair but also makes us believe that she belongs to a *culture* that grants her weight and shares in her feelings.

The unusual circumstances and characters that abound in García Márquez's fiction lead us into fully formed worlds that have an incantatory effect on the reader. Indeed, one of the sources of the mainstream success of García Márquez is that he seems to depart from the self-reflective mode so prevalent in other Latin American writing.[2] But is there an intention to go "beyond fiction" implied throughout his work? How might we delineate a critical moment in texts that are, apparently, so refractory to any purpose but the pleasure of being read?

One Hundred Years of Solitude, García Márquez's best-known book, offers several answers to these questions. One of them is optimistic; the reader closes the book without feeling that its plot is an obstacle to critical thought, because of the conceit of a manuscript being deciphered at the end.³ The story told in the novel leads us through several generations of the Buendía family, including the exploits of male characters whose names are repeated in such a way that we find it hard to differentiate them, and the lives of their wives and female associates, whose remarkable characteristics give them an individuality lost among their male counterparts.

The town of Macondo, where most of the novel takes place, is a self-enclosed community. As we read the book, without taking into account the ending, we have the impression that we know everything about it; the notion that there is only one mystery that is not revealed reinforces our sense that we have had access to whatever else constitutes the stock of information we need:

One September afternoon, with the threat of a storm, he returned home earlier than usual. He greeted Rebeca in the dining room, tied the dogs up in the courtyard, hung the rabbits up in the kitchen to be salted later, and went to the bedroom to change his clothes. Rebeca later declared that when her husband went into the bedroom she was locked in the bathroom and did not hear anything. It was a difficult version to believe, but there was no other more plausible, and no one could think of any motive for Rebeca to murder a man who had made her happy. That was perhaps the only mystery that was never cleared up in Macondo. As soon as José Arcadio closed the bedroom door, the sound of a pistol echoed through the house. (p. 129)

The movements of José Arcadio as he entered the house, the enumeration of the small tasks involved in his getting ready to turn in for the night, create a sense of familiarity. The mystery of his death is an occasion for making us part of its opposite: the daily chores of his life. Even the way in which the characters learn of his demise has the physicality of a "real" fact:

A trickle of blood came out under the door, crossed the living room, went out into the street, continued on in a straight line across the uneven terraces, went down steps and climbed over curbs, passed along the Street of the Turks, turned a corner to the right and another to the left, made a right angle at the Buendía house, went in under the closed door, crossed through the parlor, hugging the walls so as not to stain the rugs, went on to the other living room, made a wide curve to avoid the dining-room table, went along the porch with the begonias, and passed without being seen under Amaranta's chair as she gave an arithmetic lesson to Aureliano José, and went through the pantry and came out in the kitchen, where Úrsula was getting ready to crack thirty-six eggs to make bread. (pp. 129–30)

In an early book, before the rift in their friendship, Mario Vargas Llosa suggests that there is a kind of deicide attempted in the literature of García Márquez.⁴ His desire to build and control these individual and highly populated worlds seems to him a sort of assumption by the writer of the functions ascribed to God. Whether we agree or not with Vargas Llosa's formulation, the disconcerting faithfulness of detail devoted to fictional enclosures is, indeed, the most salient trait of García Márquez's writing. We do not know who committed the murder, or even if it was a murder, but the space in which it took place draws us intensely into participating with the characters in a daily existence ordered differently from our own.

Projection is, then, the prevailing attitude in a first reading of *One Hundred Years of Solitude*. But the hypothesis of the whole novel having a manuscript that is being deciphered at the end produces the general effect of reweaving everything we have read from the very beginning. Considered from this perspective, the ending of the novel is nostalgic; the story of the Buendía family is over, and the reader is made to leave the scene of projection with the awareness that no continuation is possible, given the apocalyptic ending of the book:

> Before reaching the final line, however, he had already understood that he would never leave that room, for it was foreseen that the city of mirrors (or mirages) would be wiped out by the wind and exiled from the memory of men at the precise moment when Aureliano Babilonia would finish deciphering the parchments, and that everything written on them was unrepeatable since time immemorial and forever more, because races condemned to one hundred years of solitude did not have a second opportunity on earth. (p. 383)

With the loss of the reader's innocence—not only is the novel a fiction, but the very volume he is holding in his hands has a questionable integrity—detachment becomes possible. The abandonment of the naive stage of reading is worked into the novel in two strands: the ending is the demise of the Buendía family, which constitutes the plot, and the *beginning* of critical awareness, through the notion of a manuscript that holds all clues for understanding. Thus *One Hundred Years of Solitude* closes asking the reader to recover from the dizziness of fiction. The remedy is conceived in the form of an exercise in literary interpretation, stemming from the recognition that the plot has been filtered by a dubious translation.[5]

One Hundred Years of Solitude takes issue with other writers' contempt for plot and celebrates literary interpretation as a way *out* of its illusions *within* the confines of the novel. A totalizing intention underlies the project conceived from this perspective. In an earlier formulation of the issue as it appears in an exemplary way in Cortázar's *Hopscotch,* the reader would choose between two difficult avenues of pursuit: the delight in the linear sequence of events, with "La Maga" as a central node of meaning, or the disjointed critical perspective stemming from Morelli's notes.[6]

One Hundred Years of Solitude masks the seams of its fiction until that crucial moment, the ending of the book, where they become, in turn, the decisive instance in the materiality of what is being read. In another figuration of Borges's *Aleph*, the events of the book are portrayed as being embodied in an instant:

> The final projection, which Aureliano had begun to glimpse when he let himself be confused by the love of Amaranta Úrsula, was based on the fact that Melquíades had not put events in the order of man's conventional time but had concentrated a century of daily episodes in such a way that they coexisted in one instant. (p. 382)

It has been noted repeatedly that this ending places the novel in the long tradition of self-reflective literature. But is this the most compelling reading of the ending of *One Hundred Years of Solitude*, or might a quite different sense of the text be elicited once the final pages are considered in context?

There may not be a book within this book. What we are reading is an Aleph, such is the hypothesis we would entertain, prompting speculation as to what an ideal reading of this volume might be, according to its own terms.

The Intelligent Reader

When Aureliano, the decipherer, alone in the room, finds the clues to the interpretation of the manuscript, he is forced to dismiss actively another aspect of his situation:

> Wounded by the fatal lances of his own nostalgia and that of others, he admired the persistence of the spider-webs on the dead rose bushes, the perseverance of the rye grass, the patience of the air in the radiant February dawn. And then he saw the child. It was a dry and bloated bag of skin that all the ants in the world were dragging toward their holes along the stone path in the garden. Aureliano could not move. Not because he was paralyzed by horror but because at that prodigious instant Melquíades' final keys were revealed to him . . . (p. 381)

Thus the interpreter's task is rooted in an act of oblivion so violent that his gesture can hardly attempt to be all-embracing. In "The Aleph," the protagonist ends up relegating to forgetfulness the all-encompassing object in order to go on with his life. In *One Hundred Years of Solitude*, Aureliano is engulfed by his interest in the manuscript—a cipher of his own past—and forgets about the immediate destiny of his offspring. The initial confidence in the affirmation of the rereading of the novel construed as Melquíades's elusive truth disappears, giving way to the gap separating the time of interpretation from the present tense, the urgency of pain.

A recognition of this gap locates interpretation in a temporal sequence, in which looking into the past becomes, paradoxically, simultaneous with forgetting the facts constituting it. The dismissal of the very level of experience it attempts to elucidate brackets the authenticity of its intentions as it uncovers the fictionality of the deciphering of the book within the book through a reading distrustful of the dialectical illusions offered by the novel. The conceit of the book within the book in *One Hundred Years of Solitude* thus produces the figure of a reader-decipherer who, from within fiction, is charged with giving shape to events leading to his own inception as a character. His intelligence is not without bounds, however. The outer limit of its reach is indicated with precision in the dismissal of the immediate events that comprise the concrete conditions for the act of interpretation.

Although the decipherer incarnates the most recognizable figure for the act of reading in the novel, another character of a different sort embodies the qualities attributable to the materiality of fiction itself. A striking young woman, known in the novel as Remedios the Beauty, provides us with elements that help us elucidate the notions of intelligence at work in *One Hundred Years of Solitude*.

Remedios has an evanescent presence. The nature of her intelligence is a lively source of discussion for the other characters, who are divided in their opinions about her. There are those who think that she is retarded or merely stupid, yet others, such as the Colonel Aureliano Buendía, believe she has a special lucidity that makes traditional modes of thought dispensable.[7]

The nature of the passion she ignites in the males who pursue her causes the reader to view her as the ever-elusive object of a desire destined to remain unsatisfied. Remedios evokes a long literary tradition in which female beauty is portrayed as dangerous and ultimately fatal to those who succumb to its spell. *One Hundred Years of Solitude* conveys her as a tragicomic character, with parodical overtones:

Remedios the Beauty gave off a breath of perturbation, a tormenting breeze that was still perceptible several hours after she had passed by. Men expert in the disturbances of love, experienced all over the world, stated that they had never suffered an anxiety similar to the one produced by the natural smell of Remedios the Beauty. On the porch with the begonias, in the parlor, in any place in the house, it was possible to point out the exact place where she had been and the time that had passed since she had left it. (p. 218)

Remedios's speech, unschooled in metaphor, uses a literality occasionally hilarious in its effects. Remedios is larger than life but expresses, as a fictional figure, an intensity that stands for the notion of reality itself. Her presence has an extreme carnality. One of the arguments against her intelligence is that she does not like to wear clothes. Her lightly clad body is a constant reminder of her ahistorical nature, because her refusal to participate in culture places her either above or beneath it. As the novel evolves, Remedios levitates away, leaving behind a nostalgia for solving the doubts she inspired.

There is an unknown quality about Remedios. The unfolding of her enigma recalls the way in which Melquíades's prophecy is deciphered. Her eloquence may be mistaken for lack of intelligent speech because of the inadequacy of her language in the context of everyday conversation.[8]

Melquíades's manuscript remains virtually invisible until a revelatory moment sets the deciphering in motion; in very much the same way, Remedios's lucidity is accessible through an act of belief in the sophistication of her mind. The instantaneous perception of her beauty invests her carnality with a nondiscursive meaning. Thus her literal use of language turns, in the minds of some, into the invention of a series of wise aphorisms. Remedios richly encapsulates everything that may be said about the representational level in the novel that is conceivable as a grounding for its fictional weave. Remedios seems to exist in a deeper context, beyond words, as a privileged representative of the literary tradition preceding the novel, a powerful entity precipitating changes in the destinies of others by her mere presence.

The other female characters are partial embodiments of the mystery of Remedios. They share with her the capacity for hiding part of their motivations, the design that portrays them as being part of a world of secrets. Such are the traits of Amaranta, Amaranta Úrsula, Pilar Ternera, Rebeca, and Fernanda, who remain unknown to the reader despite the many anecdotes they help develop. The nature of their secret is, perhaps, their femaleness, and is seen as constituting a potential danger to other characters who belong to the more recognizable world of adventure, where action is the measure of time. Aside from the inevitable considerations linking this representation of women to ideologies of the eternal feminine, it is worth noting that their power lies in their lack of participation in the discursive world of the other characters.

The reasons for the kind of gravitational power they each exercise are varied: Fernanda has a mysterious ailment and, like Rebeca, a past unknown to the reader; Úrsula sees through her blindness and intuition beyond any explanation about the sources of her power; Pilar Ternera's physical energy is to be matched only by nature itself; Amaranta has an uncanny apathy that endows her with a patience invested in obsessive plotting; Amaranta Úrsula is a combination of the two female characters present in her name. Her powers are enormous and her physical energy is portrayed as almost impersonal because of its similarity to a "natural" force. This rapid inventory of traits provides the register in which Remedios becomes an emblem for understanding the role that this privileged energy plays in the assessment of how the novel works. These female characters possess something beyond intelligence; they have ways of understanding and interacting with what appears as a leap, in which the rational, though acknowledged, is always marginalized.

Remedios is the hyperbolic figuration of the process that turns these female characters into sources of a secret energy. When she levitates out of the novel, Remedios intensifies the kind of nostalgia created by the other women in the novel. Her loss is the loss of the potential existence of a reality that was possible because of the carnality with which her presence was rendered persuasively to the reader.

Melquíades's manuscript is an object attuned to the nature of Remedios. Its language is not discursive and sequential, although it is rich in effects sustaining the desire to understand it. Remedios may not be part of this world, but her otherworldliness precipitates other characters to a fatal end. The manuscript to be deciphered has, like the love generated by Remedios, a frightening capacity for causing violence.

The solitary decipherer, Aureliano, forgets about his own child as he starts to understand Melquíades's message. Paradoxically, by forgetting his offspring he has the hope of finding himself:

> Fascinated by the discovery, Aureliano read aloud without skipping the chanted encyclicals that Melquíades himself had made Arcadio listen to and that were in reality the prediction of his execution, and he found the announcement of the birth of the most beautiful woman in the world who was rising up to heaven in body and soul, and he found the origin of the posthumous twins who gave up deciphering the parchments, not simply through incapacity and lack of drive, but also because their attempts were premature. At that point, impatient to know his own origin, Aureliano skipped ahead. (p. 382)

He skips ahead. Aureliano's "intelligent" reading feeds on partiality. As a character, he portrays a kind of reader who does not facilitate our own projection in him as we go through the novel. Aureliano strives to find himself through the betrayal of two poles that sustain the fiction in which he participates.

As he forgets his offspring he becomes unfaithful to the layer of plot that might grant him a future as a member of an extinct family. The refusal to perform the funeral rites for his son constitutes the objective ending of his adventures.

The implicit reader of *One Hundred Years of Solitude* is betrayed by Aureliano's lack of interest in following every avatar of the manuscript.

As he skips passages so that he may find his own origins, he ceases to be a neutral embodiment of reading to become, more explicitly, what he has always been: a fictional character whose limitations represent the consequences of hedonistic self-interest.

What Are We Reading?

By conceiving of Aureliano as an "intelligent" decipherer and Remedios as the embodiment of a nondiscursive enigma, we have constituted the basic scene of reading and writing: the reader (Aureliano), on the one hand, and the subject (Remedios), on the other. The stability of this arrangement disappears with the emergence of Aureliano's unfaithful reading, because the will to partiality as a means of self-understanding returns him to the same level as the other characters in the novel. What is the proper way of annotating that level? We must ask, moreover, what is entailed by the question itself. In attempting to answer it, we should rephrase it so as to question the place of the reader in the novel, since the awareness of a shared ground necessitates our finding another point of departure for the critical reading. García Márquez has taken up this issue and elaborated further on its many reverberations in later works.

The Autumn of the Patriarch,[9] a novel written with a texture that approximates a prose poem, presents a Latin American dictator with recognizable traits drawn from the history of various countries. Dense and repetitive images introduce the complex underpinnings of his power. The dictator's absolute authority stems, to a large extent, from his capacity to draw on the mystery that his persona has created. The issue of whether he is dead or alive is discussed by "the people." The unpredictability of his reactions grants him a specificity that intensifies the sense that his being is beyond the grasp of the common person. His government is sustained by a complicated system of staged illusions; the substantial presence attained by the dictator in the eyes of his contemporaries is shown from inside as a machine of conventions that produces power as an artifice.

In the midst of the jubilant bell-ringing, the festival rockets, the music of celebration with which the laying of the first stone of reconstruction was laid, and in the midst of the shouts of the multitude crowded into the main square to glorify the most worthy one who had put the hurricane dragon to flight, someone took him by the arm to lead him out into the balcony because now more than ever the people needed his words of comfort, and before he could get away he heard the unanimous clamor which got into his innards like the wind of an evil sea, long live the stud, because ever since the first days of his regime he understood the unprotected state of being seen by a whole city at the same time, his words turned to stone, he understood in a flash of mortal lucidity that he did not have the courage nor would he ever have it to appear at full length before the chasm of the crowd, so on the main square we only caught sight of the usual ephemeral image, the glimpse of an ungraspable old man dressed in denim who imparted a silent blessing from the presidential balcony and immediately disappeared. (p. 98)

The dictator is described as "being all alone," "deaf as a mirror," a dubious lover, and a fleeting presence for "the people." He bans his own mother from the presidential mansion for her meager historical sense when she confirms his lack of education by stating that, had she known the heights to which he would rise, she would have sent him to school. Aside from the situational humor and the abundant social comment that may be drawn from the mother's statement, we should reflect on how the dictator is given the attributes of a triumphant will shorn of all intelligence.

The texture of the novel allows the reader to see two strands of the repressive tapestry woven by the dictatorship: one is the ruthless violence exercised against the opposition, replete with shifts in motives for striking out at hastily defined enemies; the other is the thread that seams the dictator's image together for "the people" to behold.[10]

What are the tricks that shape the dictator for the outside world? A suspicion of repeated doublings conceal his own identity; his speeches, composed of clichés, save him from the travails of originality in language; his lovesickness for a female character who spurns him with her final disappearance grants him a sense of humanity, insofar as she represents the beauty of the poor ("la belleza del muladar") and the kind of vulnerability often associated with demagogy.

The dictator is an elusive object whose language and being are a subject of interpretation. *The Autumn of the Patriarch* raises, in a different framework, the problem of how to interpret the presence of a character who, devoid of intelligence, nevertheless precipitates the most important events in the narrative. Because he lacks an analytical mind, the dictator is an ideal subject for analysis. His silence—like Remedios's unschooled speech in *One Hundred Years of Solitude*—triggers the need for speaking in others.

The Autumn of the Patriarch is an extended meditation on the authority granted to a character because of ignorance of his origins and life; the less readers know about the reasons determining him, the more attracted they are to study him and fall within his aura. The illusion of depth that such a development gives to fiction is seen in the novel through its political aspect of cruelty as well as its playful literary implications. The system that was initiated in *One Hundred Years of Solitude* reappears in *Autumn of the Patriarch,* establishing the limits of objects to be read with increased analytical clarity: the reader is drawn to a *secret*.

The dictator, Remedios, and Melquíades's manuscript offer several faces: one is an all-embracing intelligence, the other is staggering stupidity and ignorance. As in *One Hundred Years of Solitude*, *The Autumn of the Patriarch* gives readers an entity on which to project themselves. The object, however, is no longer the Buendías, but "the people," who see the dictator from afar as he passes in a car without their being certain of what his face looks like, but still being sure of the pressing nature of the question of his identity. In that partial system of projections, readers are less fortunate than they were in *One Hundred Years of Solitude*, because this time there is no way out of the reading enclosure. Although it was possible to frame Aureliano's reading of Melquíades's manuscript in a specific room and look at it from another level, the *outside*, in *The Autumn of the Patriarch* that "beyond" does not exist. For it is conceived as the world itself, and the reader is drawn from this dictator to all others, *outside* the book but *within* a society that turns mystery and stupidity into absolute authority.

Let's Work with Facts

In the short novel *Chronicle of a Death Foretold*,[11] the elusiveness of what is being told in the narrative is absent. The reader is clear about the subject from the outset. The fact is more tangible than comprehensible: a man has been murdered. The various characters are introduced through a kind of lineup, each with opinions and certainties that were not enough to stop the death from occurring.

The murder took place in the context of a tightly knit community; its motive was simple and traditional. It involved a marriage, a virginity lost by the bride at the wrong time, an explanation that may not have been true, and the death of the alleged male culprit at the hands of avenging males. Hispanic cultural tradition offers this solution as a way of clearing the tainted family's honor, which justifies the townspeople's lack of surprise at the violent resolution, since both the event and its consequences have become part of their shared experience even before they occur.

Given the profoundly *known* nature of what is being told, how does this novel produce the tension of suspense? What may the reader expect from its pages? The pleasures elicited by reading this book are closely intertwined with a celebration of reality. The murder is invested with the weight of a necessary element; it is *there*. The role of the characters in *Chronicle of a Death Foretold* is none other than to attest to the existence of the event that holds them together by making it "happen" over and over again. García Márquez's affinities with cinematography, present throughout his writing career, are particularly obvious in this work. Tangibility has replaced analytical understanding; seeing is the key to believing. Thus the reader, persuaded of the event as occurrence, ends up also convinced of its inevitability.

Common sense, with its incapacity to generate new solutions and its eminently conservative rhythm, dominates a narration that, paradoxically, grants major importance to the role of dreams and local superstitions. Faced with thinking about the murder, all characters are trapped in the destructive defense of the family's honor. Although the novel starts by stating the fact of the murder, its suspense is built on the credibility of the motives leading to its perpetration, its weight for a reader. The success of the book resides in silencing that level of reading that might want to question the event, that is, the silencing of a more intelligent and suspicious look at the information.

In García Márquez we find a passion for documentation, be it in the form of the proliferation of details that give life to Macondo in *One Hundred Years of Solitude* or the flat interviewing and reporting in *Chronicle of a Death Foretold*. His sense of writing as the transmission of facts, fictional or not, is nowhere more apparent than in *The General in His Labyrinth*,[12] a novel dealing with the last days of Simón Bolívar's life.

Like Borges in "Guayaquil," García Márquez is fascinated by the riddle of what motivated Bolívar.[13] In this case, the focus is on Bolívar's loneliness rather than the uncertainty of the documentation about him. García Márquez is not Zimerman; he does not try to interpret documents. His task in this novel is historical reconstruction, seen as unproblematic.

The General in His Labyrinth, the result of detailed research on Bolívar's period and his correspondence, shows us a physically diminished general. He is frequently feverish; his understanding of the political situation is failing, those around him are not completely faithful to him, and his sense of his own mission is subsumed by nostalgia and the ailments of age.

Bolívar is portrayed as remembering clearly swatches of music and his long romance with Manuela Sánchez.[14] The novel produces a strong local atmosphere, and its main virtue resides in the ability to recreate the flavors and sounds that Bolívar was exposed to throughout his life at the same time that it focuses on his imminent death. We find here again, as in *Autumn of the Patriarch,* the presence of "the people" as a background and eloquent testimony to the hero's authority, while the very notion of his heroism is dismantled as we learn about the concrete details of his existence.

The solitude of power is a preoccupation here, as in *Autumn of the Patriarch* and *One Hundred Years of Solitude*. The greatest emphasis, nevertheless, is on faithfulness to facts, which leads to a paradoxical result: the overabundance of documented dances, letters, and political positions is read as a more or less ornamental web.

Chronicle of a Death Foretold relinquishes its factuality in favor of highlighting the superstitions and backward clichés of the townspeople; *The General in His Labyrinth* loses the "truth" of its historical facts as the novel beckons the reader to turn attention to a more universal theme: an old man dying as he fails to understand the present and tries to revive his past. As in Borges's "Guayaquil," documents have their own way of affecting their readers, and, as in *One Hundred Years of Solitude*, a world being engulfed as it is being retold becomes the pretext for the narrative.

Scenes of Reading

In drawing the scenes of reading as they appear in each of these novels, we have found a need to distinguish between readers and reading *within fiction*, as part of a plot, and reading and readers in the sense commonly understood as *critical*. Following closely such developments in *One Hundred Years of Solitude*, we evolved a model of reading in which lucidity was equated with the mystery of Remedios's silence as a grounding for fiction, whereas a hostile reaction to Aureliano's partial interest in deciphering the past embodied the beginning of critical awareness on the part of the detached reader.

The Autumn of the Patriarch intensifies these problems by turning Remedios's eloquence and elusiveness into a haunting political problem in the figure of the dictator. *Love in the Time of Cholera*[15] presents a series of scenes of reading and writing as the very thread of its plot. Part of the charm of this novel stems from the anachronistic courtship between two elderly characters, whose romance initially appears to have been made possible by memories of their attachment during their youth, which revolved around letters from the male character, Florentino Ariza, to his female counterpart, Fermina Daza. After more than 440 pages, however, the importance granted to the epistolary link changes.

Florentino Ariza goes to Fermina's house after he has sent her a letter (not yet received) he had written in a state of depression caused by the embarrassment of his first visit to her house. The encounter runs smoothly, overcoming, in practice, the difficulties that had prompted the composition of the letter. A new system of mail delivery in town enables the letter to arrive precisely at the time that Florentino is visiting, at ease, with Fermina. He immediately decides to ask her not to read the letter.

"Of course"—(she said)—"After all, letters belong to the one who writes them, don't they?"
He stepped with decision.
"That's the way it is"—he said—"That's why they are the first things to be returned when there is a break up."
She overlooked his intention and returned the letter to him saying: "It is a pity that I can't read it, because the others were very helpful to me." He took a deep breath, amazed at the spontaneity with which she had said much more than he had expected, and told her: "You have no idea the happiness that this knowledge gives me." But she changed the subject and he could not get her to come back to it for the rest of the afternoon. (p. 446)

After having been the only real link between two characters who had been physically separate, the letters enter—through Fermina's reaction—into another realm. They become something different from the weighty reality that brought them together, something that Florentino dares define as literature:

Four days later, on Tuesday, he came back without previous notice, and she did not wait until after tea was served to tell him how much his letters had meant to her. He told her that they had not been letters in the strict sense, but loose pages from a book he would have liked to write. She had also understood them as that, so much so that she thought of returning them to him if he would not take it as a rejection, so that he could put them to a better use. (p. 446)

If the last pages of *One Hundred Years of Solitude* represent a reevaluation of the novel as a pretext for an exercise of interpretation and translation by a character, *Love in the Time of Cholera* takes two routes simultaneously: one that leads us in the direction of literature and the other, portrayed as divergent, that brings us closer to feelings seen as more "real" than the ones in the hypothetical book.

The mention of a book in progress in *Love in the Time of Cholera* serves to show that, at age seventy-two, Fermina Daza can still be a cunning reader and a blushing inspirer of courtship. Yet what would have happened if Fermina had understood the letters to be the source of their amorous link? Why is it that the proper response is to relegate them to the realm of a book in the making? Fermina returns the letters to Florentino, thereby freeing herself from the book. If the letters had remained as their true link, we know from our tradition in representing the disappointments of love that some kind of awareness of how literature could not contain the deterioration caused by the passage of time would have followed. Our era can punish two lovers who want to join in the freedom of the page through an effective call to that other side, beyond their control, represented by age, sickness, betrayal, or money.

In returning the letters and safely confining them to a book, Fermina is able to make the transition from potential gullible reader (believer in illusions, unable to take action, dreamer unconnected to the present) to credible lover. Literature has been given a place, it has served the purpose of bringing Fermina and Florentino together and now must be pushed aside so that their romance may continue.

Seduced by the letters, Fermina was, nevertheless, also capable of maintaining the kind of distance that left room for the reality of Florentino, the man, to emerge. What is Fermina's special gift? How can she separate the fanciful world of literary contests and courtship correspondence from life? Where is the source of her capacity to be enveloped by romance and yet be immune to the confusion caused by the mirage of its many conventions? A look at the description of how she furnished the house where she lived with her husband during their long marriage casts a light onto the nature of her strengths:

> The furnishings in the sitting rooms, including the pendulum clock that stood like a living sentinel in the drawing room, were all original English pieces from the late nineteenth century, and the lamps that hung from the walls were all tear-drop crystal, and there were Sevre vases and bowls everywhere as well as little alabaster statues of pagan idylls. But that European coherence vanished in the rest of the house, where wicker arm chairs were jumbled together with Viennese rockers and leather footstools made by local craftsmen. Splendid hammocks from San Jacinto, with multicolored fringe around the sides and the owner's name embroidered in Gothic letters with silk thread hung in the bedrooms along with the beds. . . . Throughout the house one could detect the good sense and care of a woman whose feet were planted firmly on the ground. (pp. 18–19)

Fermina has the steadiness of parochialism. "Tiene los pies sobre la tierra": she belongs firmly in this world. European decor gives way to the authenticity of creole furnishings; she has the wisdom of those who know their own restricted world. Fermina has common sense; there lies the source of her strength and, paradoxically, the energy that allows her to act on the love she had felt for so many years for Florentino.

Love letters for her, chapters or plans for a book in the making—Fermina does not care about the purpose of those written pages. The letters, like the imported furniture in some of her rooms, may be necessary bows to convention, but the energy behind it all is the fabric of Florentino's and Fermina's lives, portrayed as having the kind of authenticity exuded by the local furniture in her home. As in *One Hundred Years of Solitude* and other works by García Márquez, the virtues of common sense and intuition are emphasized as being particularly feminine, in contrast to their relative absence in the male characters.

Florentino's interest in literature makes him vulnerable to being victimized by it, to the extent that he was ready to suffer the consequences of taking the letters "seriously" and thereby risking his relationship with Fermina, had she not disregarded them so readily by accepting them as belonging to literature. Dr. Urbino, Fermina's longtime husband, is also portrayed as an intellectual. Although he is a solid member of the community and enjoys reading history books, he has one fanciful occupation that leads to his death.

Replicating the contrasts between the local and the imported in his house, Dr. Urbino owns pet parrots to whom he speaks in French and Spanish.[16] The novel tells us that when he was younger he had succeeded in teaching French so well to one of them that the parrot attained the command of a true scholar. One day, as Dr. Urbino is engaged in speaking Spanish to a parrot, it tries to fly away. He calls it back and then attempts to reach it by climbing a ladder. It should be noted that at this point in the novel Dr. Urbino had already passed his eightieth birthday.

> The parrot did not move and perched so close to the ground that Dr. Urbino held out his walking stick to him so that he could sit on the silver handle, as he always did, but the parrot sidestepped and went up to the next branch, a bit higher up but easier to reach since the house ladder had been leaning against it even before the arrival of the firemen. Dr. Urbino estimated the height and thought that if he climbed two rungs he would be able to catch him. He stepped onto the first singing a disarming, friendly song to entice the churlish bird who repeated the words, although not the music and continued to move farther out on the branch. He climbed to the second rung without difficulty, holding on to the ladder with both hands, and the parrot began to repeat the entire song without moving from the spot. He climbed to the third rung and then the fourth, for he had miscalculated the height of the branch, and then he grasped the ladder with his left hand and tried to seize the parrot with his right. Digna Pardo, the old servant, was coming to remind him that he would be late. . . . Dr. Urbino caught the parrot around the neck with a triumphant sigh: ca y est. But he released him immediately because the ladder slipped from under his feet and for an instant he was suspended in the air and then he realized that he had died. (pp. 41–42)

Unlike Fermina, Dr. Urbino cannot free himself from the friction generated by the two differing halves of his existence. He is literally killed by his parrot because he is unable to judge properly the distance between them. He has been, in the terms of the Kafkian creature evoked by Borges in *The Book of Imaginary Beings*, thoroughly "tamed" by his disconcertingly language-proficient bird. His death is a testimony of defeat in battle. Fermina's expertise is the result of a fundamental lack of interest in the conventions of art, literature, and the intellect. Closer to the parrot than to Florentino or Dr. Urbino, Fermina stands for a beyond language that makes the story, also perceived as life, flow.

Fermina and Florentino are described as carrying the scent of old age in their bodies, at a time of sickness and death. Nevertheless, they are made to embody the ideal of youthful passion as they remain true to the intensity of their early liaison, decades before the final union that constitutes the subject of the novel. This resolution is made possible under the aegis of a refusal of literature.

In *One Hundred Years of Solitude* the explicit ending of the novel points the reading toward a disregard for the avatars of the Buendía family in favor of the hypothesis of a manuscript being unfolded and in urgent need of elucidation. Critical elucidation rather than the multiple projections in plot is asserted as the purpose of both reading and writing. *Love in the Time of Cholera* works toward an opposite effect. The hypothetical book being written through Florentino's letters is made to be a mere moment—to be disregarded—in the couple's "true story." The accent here is on the notion that what is crucial in the narrative is experience.

Is this dichotomy accurate? Should we posit that critical interpretation is to be distinguished as the opposite of life-imitating narratives? The answer given by *Love in the Time of Cholera* demands a double effort on our part: on the one hand, leave aside the book, close it; on the other, allow Florentino and Fermina to live out for us, through the denial of the book, an intense romance with a coherence that we can only associate with literature, though this time of a different sort.

When Jacob's wife (in the epigraph to this chapter) says that she wishes to be buried alive, we are startled into the recognition that we are entering a world complete with desires, anxieties, and unknown adversities. Still, her voice has the echoes of small-town gossip, and we can visualize her despair and, in an oblique manner, share it. The separate world of the story beckons for us to enter it by assuming complicities and sharing its intricacies.

García Márquez's work plays the unfamiliar so that it may become commonsensical. His narratives are permeated by the will of completeness, frequently ending apocalyptically. Whether it is the unfolding of scenes of reading and writing, or the careful search for reality through historical reconstruction, such as in *The General in His Labyrinth*; political synthesis, as in *The Autumn of the Patriarch*; or journalistic technique, as in *Chronicle of a Death Foretold,* the purpose is to expose and complete mangled messages.

What kind of intelligence is needed to participate aptly in García

Márquez's worlds? The question is posed and responded to in divergent ways through his writing: pleasure, faithfulness to intuition, and an affinity for the tangible are privileged in his work. Whether they are ultimately triumphant over critical intelligence depends on our own luck in the battle with Dr. Urbino's parrot.

Notes

1. Gabriel García Márquez, *Innocent Erendira and Other Stories*, trans. Gregory Rabassa (New York: Harper and Row, 1978), pp. 60–61. For the connections between this story and children's literature, see Joel Hancock, "Gabriel García Márquez's Erendira and the Brothers Grimm," *Studies in Twentieth Century Literature* 3, 1 (1978): 45–52.

2. For a general view of critical perspectives on this author, see Bernard McGuirk and Richard Cardwell, *Gabriel García Márquez: New Readings* (Cambridge: Cambridge University Press, 1987). García Márquez is also a prolific journalist who, because of the mainstream interest in his literary and political opinions, has been interviewed frequently. Among the best such sources are Plinio Apuleyo Mendoza, *El olor de la guayaba* (Barcelona: Bruguera, 1982), Ernesto González Bermejo, "Ahora doscientos años de soledad," *Triunfo* 441 (1970): 12–18, and Alfonso Rentería Mantilla, ed., *García Márquez habla de García Márquez: 33 reportajes* (Bogotá: Rentería, 1979).

3. Gabriel García Márquez, *Cien años de soledad* (Buenos Aires: Editorial Sudamericana, 1967). Quotations are from the English translation by Gregory Rabassa, *One Hundred Years of Solitude* (New York: Harper and Row, 1970, reprint Avon, 1974). Julio Ortega studies the intricacies of this novel from a perspective that illustrates its early reception. See Julio Ortega, "Gabriel García Márquez: *Cien años de soledad*," in his book *La contemplación y la fiesta: Ensayos sobre la nueva novela latinoamericana* (Lima: Editorial Universitaria, 1968). The collected volume edited by Helmy F. Giacoman, *Homenaje a Gabriel García Márquez* (Long Island City, N.Y.: Las Américas, 1972), and Wolfgang A. Luchting's "Gabriel García Márquez: The Boom and the Whimper," *Books Abroad* 44 (Winter 1970): 26–30, are testimonies of the extent to which García Márquez became not only a renowned author but also an *event*. Emir Rodríguez Monegal, shrewd student as well as one of the main contributors to the construction of the so-called boom of Latin American fiction, perceived early on what would become the main critical issue in the discussion of *One Hundred Years of Solitude*. See Emir Rodríguez Monegal, "*One Hundred Years of Solitude*, the Last Three Pages," *Books Abroad* 47 (1973): 485–89.

4. Mario Vargas Llosa, *Gabriel García Márquez: Historia de un deicidio* (Barcelona: Seix Barral, 1971). See also Mario Vargas Llosa, "García Márquez: From Aracataca to Macondo," *Review* 70 (1971): 129–42.

5. The device is already present in Cervantes; some of its consequences are studied in Chapter 2 herein, devoted to Jorge Luis Borges. For an interpretation of the sense of history in the novel, see Djelal Kadir, "The Architectonic Principle of *Cien años de soledad* and the Vichian Theory of History," *Kentucky Romance Quarterly* 24, 3 (1977): 251–61.

6. See Chapter 4 devoted to Julio Cortázar, for a full development of the topic.

7. Isaac Bashevis Singer explores the peculiar intelligence suggested by a woman's mental retardation in his novel *Shosha*. Shosha's lack of understanding of a certain logical dimension enables her to serve as an embodiment of a profound and lost Jewish world. The closeness that Remedios has to more "basic" experiences has affinities with Singer's character. In addition, Clarice Lispector has explored throughout her work women's absent-mindedness as an alternate focus that allows for privileged experiences. The stories collected in *Family Ties* are a good example of her unblinking treatment of the subject. See Clarice Lispector, *Family Ties* (Austin: University of Texas Press, 1972). García Márquez's perspective on the subject through the character of Remedios is humorous and lighter than the approach encountered in either Lispector or Singer.

8. Remedios is presented as both a comic and a serious character. She remains ambiguous throughout the novel, suggesting García Márquez's own ambivalence about the exaggerated femininity she represents. In "The Smallest Woman in the World," Clarice Lispector parodies the ideal of the innocent sexuality of an unknowing female, shifting the capacities of love from the male to the female with disconcerting results. See Lispector, *Family Ties,* pp. 88–95.

9. Gabriel García Márquez, *El otoño del patriarca* (Buenos Aires: Editorial Sudamericana, 1975). I quote from Gregory Rabassa's translation, *The Autumn of the Patriarch* (New York: Avon, 1977). Graciela Palau de Nemes points out the direct historical references present in the novel in her "Gabriel García Márquez: *El otoño del patriarca,*" *Hispamérica* 4, 11–12 (1975): 172–83. See also on the same subject Angel Rama's "Un patriarca en la remozada galería de dictadores," *Eco* 29, 178 (1975): 408–43, and Raymond L. Williams, "The Dynamic Structure of García Márquez's *El otoño del patriarca,*" *Symposium* 32 (Spring 1978): 56–75.

10. Augusto Roa Bastos's *Yo, el supremo* (Buenos Aires: Siglo XXI, 1975) and Alejo Carpentier's *El recurso del método* (Buenos Aires: Siglo XXI, 1974) consider the same subject, forming a sort of trilogy with García Márquez's novel. The joint reading of these works delineates a meditation about power in Latin America that uncovers the machinery of conventions that make it possible. Dictators are made into ideal novelistic characters here, even while they are described as ruthless, cruel, or barely alive. Michael Palencia Roth, in his *Gabriel García Márquez* (Madrid: Gredos, 1983), studies the process by which the patriarch becomes a myth in *The Autumn of the Patriarch*. See Roth's chapter entitled "El mundo del patriarca," pp. 164–263.

11. Gabriel García Márquez, *Crónica de una muerte anunciada* (Bogotá: Editorial La Oveja Negra, 1981), trans. Gregory Rabassa, *Chronicle of a Death Foretold* (New York: Knopf, 1983). See A. M. Penuel, "The Sleep of Vital Reason in García Márquez's *Crónica de una muerte anunciada,*" *Hispania* 68 (December 1985): 753–66.

12. Gabriel García Márquez, *El general en su laberinto* (Madrid: Mondadori, 1989). This concern is also evident in his book *La aventura de Miguel Littín clandestino en Chile* (Buenos Aires: Editorial Sudamericana, 1986).

13. See Chapter 2, devoted to Borges.

14. Victor W. von Hagen tells the story of this romance in a detailed historical novel that he claims is the result of thorough historical documentation. The figure of Manuela Sánchez emerging from that account is one of courage and firm political determination. In 1822, the year of her first meeting with Bolívar, she was in her mid-twenties and had already distinguished herself in

fighting against the Spaniards. See Victor W. von Hagen, *The Four Seasons of Manuela* (London: J. M. Dent and Sons, 1952).

15. Gabriel García Márquez, *El amor en los tiempos del cólera* (Barcelona: Bruguera, 1985), trans. Edith Grossman, *Love in the Time of Cholera* (London: Penguin Books, 1988). My pagination corresponds to the English edition; in some cases I have modified Grossman's translation slightly.

16. Such cultural contrasts appear elsewhere in García Márquez's work. Pietro Crespi, in *One Hundred Years of Solitude*, brings European music to the Buendía house. The toys and the pianola that he gets for the Buendía household represent a dimension different from the rural realities of Macondo. Pietro Crespi's death is the triumph of the rural over the urban, announcing Dr. Urbino's destiny.

Chapter 4
Literature as Risk: Julio Cortázar

> Because despite all that has been said about Borges's Buenos Aires—a fantastic, invented Buenos Aires—that Buenos Aires does exist but it is far from being all that the city is. Arlt perceived things from below for cultural, vital, and professional reasons and saw a Buenos Aires to live and stroll through, to love in and suffer in, while Borges saw a Buenos Aires of mythic destinies, of a metaphysical mother and eternity. So, you see, my place in that generation—which is not mine but the previous one—at the same time fulfills a moral, ethical obedience to Borges's great lesson and a telluric, sensual, erotic (as you like) obedience to Roberto Arlt.
> —Julio Cortázar, interview with Evelyn Picón Garfield[1]

The Open Book and Its Hoaxes

When Julio Cortázar places himself under the twofold tutelage of Borges and Roberto Arlt, he is trying to reconcile what he sees as the halves of a world. Borges and Arlt, in his view, have had only partial access to Buenos Aires; he is the one who, feeling the contamination of one half by the other, is prompted to write a literature that will render Buenos Aires complete. Cortázar's view is that literature should be about depicting the privileged cities, the walks and their rhythm, because through the intense experience of living with an openness to chance, the words to bring the reader in as a companion will emerge.

Hopscotch takes place in two principal cities: Paris and Buenos Aires, Cortázar's main literary and vital resources. When *Hopscotch* first appeared in 1968, it dazzled common readers and fellow writers.[2] Its requirement of at least two readings—a linear one in which the thread of a plot might be followed, and another that has the reader skipping chapters in moves that defy continuity—animates a book that is at once a vast playground, a testing ground for theories about art and literature, a traditional narrative of love and death, and an artifact whose completeness is open to observation and interrogation. From this perspective, *Hopscotch* would appear to realize the French-Uruguayan poet Comte de Lautréamont's dream of a literature written by everybody.

The active involvement of a vigilant reader is a practical response to blind habits of thought and a return to play as a source of knowledge. *Hopscotch* also rewrites literary history, offering fresh views of misunderstood or unjustly forgotten writers, among them Macedonio Fernandez, Alfred Jarry, and Felisberto Hernández. The table of instructions in *Hopscotch* formulated a dazzling future for Latin American literature; through the hospitality of that book, authors such as José Lezama Lima and Octavio Paz were joined in a realm that need not tell whether it was literature or experience, strewn with posters, abandoned umbrellas, and mirrors. *Hopscotch* accomplishes what remained only a project for the French Surrealists and serves to show us how little they delved within their own vision.[3]

The cosmopolitanism and irreverence of *Hopscotch* established the right to a profoundly antiaristocratic use of European and Argentine cultural traditions; *Hopscotch* is a web of cultural interconnections, a vote of confidence for the aimless walks of exiles in foreign cities, and the delineation of a continuum between lovemaking and the search for knowledge. Its gift to readers feeds on their capacity for surprise in the exercise of their freedom. *Hopscotch* is, thus, a landmark book that has changed the way we perceive literature before and after its publication; its lessons are now already part of our practice of reading and it becomes possible to ask how, indeed, do we read *Hopscotch* after *Hopscotch*?

Literary Reception as a Novelistic Hypothesis: Morelli/Trepat

Chapter 73 of *Hopscotch* contains one of the book's frequent reflections about literature:

How often I wonder whether this is only writing, in an age where we run towards deception through infallible equations and conformity machines. But to ask one's self if we will know how to find the other side of habit or if it's better to let one's self be borne along by its happy cybernetics, is that not literature again? Rebellion, conformity, anguish, earthly sustenance, all the dichotomies: the Yin and the Yang, contemplation or the *Tätigkeit*, oatmeal or partridge *faisandée*, Lascaux or Mathieu, what a hammock of words, what purse-size dialectics with pajama storms and living-room cataclysms. (pp. 318–19)[4]

Hopscotch is traversed by a profound disappointment with literature: "Is that not literature again?" It is as though the book tried to cancel its own words through the reading arrangement and the hypothesis of the game of hopscotch, allowing them to say something different. The reception of the book is discussed throughout, taking into account that the weaknesses inseparable from its own nature conspire against its being anything else but words.

Paradoxically, the most intellectual characters in *Hopscotch* turn out to be the least prepared for undertaking the challenges it proposes. La Maga, a female character who infuses interest in reading the novel for plot, is granted a more ready access to the privileged depth of reality. *Hopscotch* denigrates literature as vicarious experience even as it looks with antipathy toward the projection into the book as though it were reality.

The characters avidly exchange information about exhibits, films, and records, and in talking about them end up defining themselves. The results they expect from their conversations are something beyond a mere inclusion in culture. It is not enough to have seen *Potemkin* or to have read a particular book; the characters want to appropriate the words and images, tearing them away from their context and escaping with them onto the streets and into their lives, erasing the differences between producers and consumers.

Some characters are thus overtaken by certain books, phrases, or images. Art and literature are incorporated as experience. If that is the case, why be concerned about words being nothing but literature? What does it mean to be nothing but literature? As compared to what else? Horacio, the character who most embodies the doubts and ambitions of the intellectuals, provides insight into the kind of abyss opened up by these questions:

> But I'm alone in my room, I'm falling into tricks of writing, the black bitches get their vengeance any way they can, they are biting me from underneath the table. Do you say *underneath* or *under*? They bite you just the same. Why, why, *pourquoi, por que, warum, perche* this horror of black bitches? Look at them, in that poem by Nashe transformed into bees. And there in two lines from Octavio Paz, thighs of the sun, corners of the summer. But the same body of a woman belongs to Mary and to La Brinviliers, eyes that cloud up looking at a beautiful sunset are the same optical instrument that gets pleasure of the twisting of a man being hanged. I'm afraid of that pimping, of ink and of voices, a sea of tongues licking the ass of the world. There's milk and honey underneath your tongue. . . . Yes, but it's also been said that dead flies make the perfumer's perfume stink. At war with words, at war, keep everything that might be necessary even though intelligence must be renounced, stick with the simple act of ordering some fried potatoes, and Reuters dispatches, in letters from my noble brother and movie dialogues. (p. 349)

The "beyond" of literature is conceived as the black bitches, a realm of fear, on the one hand, and common sense through Reuters dispatches and a brother, on the other. Thus the refusal of literature in *Hopscotch* does not entail embracing its opposites.

Reading and writing are deemed insufficient because they represent a domesticated insertion into the world. Nevertheless, most of the characters evoked in the novel live and are consumed by their intellectual pursuits; they try to model their behavior according to an interpretation of a few pages, a film, an exhibit. Literature and art have an urgency for them that transcends the contingent objects in which they are embodied.

The fear of staying in the realm of mere literature is a commonplace of contemporary Latin American literature. In *Hopscotch* the uncomfortable relationship with the book is rendered in ways that separate it from the basic realization of the relative triviality of the written word compared with the complexity, violence, and moral challenges faced by our cultural present. *Hopscotch* tries to do away with fiction as sedative, with the aesthetic in its barbiturate and antiseptic modes. When a fictive author in the novel, Morelli, formulates his theory for a novel of the future in Chapter 62, his foremost enemy is psychology, which he sees as instituting a need for verisimilitude complicit with the tyranny of habit, stimulating the patterns of behavior based on a belief in the individual self.

Morelli, echoing Macedonio Fernández, wants to dismantle the notion that causality is an adequate tool for explaining behavior; he tries to undermine the unity of characters with strong selves. His alternative, later developed in the novel *62: A Model Kit*,[5] is that

> Everything would be a kind of disquiet, a continuous uprooting, a territory where psychological causality would yield disconcertedly, and those puppets would destroy each other without suspecting too much that life is trying to change its key in and through and by them, that a barely conceivable attempt is born in man as one other day there were being born the reason-key, the feeling-key, the pragmatism-key. That after each successive defeat there is an approach towards the final mutation, and that man only is in that he searches to be, plans to be, thumbing through words and modes of behavior and joy sprinkled with blood and other rhetorical pieces like this one. (pp. 305–6)

There is a certain optimism for the future of literature in this fragment of a quotation attributed to Morelli. Even though Morelli has an antagonistic attitude to literature as it is and has been, he hints that a human and literary transformation is possible and that we have the capacity to bring it about. Morelli's antipsychologism is bracketed, however, when, following the table of instructions provided by the novel, we skip from chapter 62 to chapter 23.

In Chapter 23, Horacio is walking in Paris on a very rainy day. When it starts pouring hard he retreats to a concert hall for shelter. The pianist, Berthe Trepat,[6] plays to an almost nonexistent audience works composed by herself and her disciple, Rose Bob. A master of ceremonies gives the following description of the pieces.

He would sum up their art by mentioning antistructural constructions, that is to say, autonomous cells of sound, the result of pure inspiration, held together by the general intent of the work, but completely free of classical modes, dodecaphonic or atonal (he stressed the last two words). Thus, for example, the *Three Discontinuous Movements* by Rose Bob, one of Madame Trepat's favorite students, had their start in the reaction aroused in the spirit of the composer by the sound of a door being slammed shut, and the thirty-two chords which make up the first movement were the resulting repercussions of that sound on the aesthetic plane; the speaker did not think he would be violating a confidence if he told his cultured audience that the technique employed in the composition of the *Saint Saëns Synthesis* was based on the most primitive and esoteric forces of creation. (p. 92)

Berthe Trepat and her disciple are avant-garde artists, but does their project not have close affinities with Morelli's theory of representation in Chapter 62, one skip back, in the very part of the novel that sent us to this one? What separates Morelli from these musical artists? Chapter 62 has not won its antipsychologizing battle. The walk that takes Horacio to his fortuitous encounter with Berthe Trepat has the necessity of the arbitrariness praised by the Surrealists, and repeats Morelli's formulation in a different register.

Berthe Trepat is described as ridiculous, and even disgusting:

Berthe Trepat looked at the audience once more, all the sins of the moon seemed suddenly concentrated in her face that appeared to be covered with flour, and her cherry-red mouth opened up to assume the shape of an Egyptian barge. Profile once again, her little parrot-beak nose pointed for a moment at the keyboard while her hands perched on the keys from C to B like two dried-up chamois bags. (p. 93)

The pages describing her interaction with Horacio reinforce the grotesque in her, emphasizing her lack of beauty and advanced age with an intensity that implies a connection between those shortcomings and her talent as an artist.

Berthe Trepat embodies a familiar figure in the misogynistic tradition: the ugly older woman with artistic or intellectual ambitions and a failure in every aspect of her life.[7] *Hopscotch* takes us further in this direction when it tells us that the man she lives with, Valentin, prefers males to females and even entertains his lovers while Berthe Trepat is left waiting outside, in the street. This implacably aggressive portrait of a female is found elsewhere in Cortázar. The fear of feminine sexual desire at work in his representation of Trepat is also present in Frau

Marta of *62: A Model Kit,* in the women who end up doing away with the artist they admire in the story "The 'Menads," and in the portrayal of the singers in the story "The Band," to list but a few examples.[8] The humiliation that Horacio experiences in his contact with Trepat, together with the enumeration of her circumstances and appearance, qualify Trepat's will to artistic fulfillment.

The emphasis on her as a *character* makes us think of her art as a consequence of her life; the transgressive character of her artistic project is merely one more trait in her general physiognomy. "Parrot-beak nose," hands like "two dried-up chamois bags," "original" compositions . . . Trepat is exasperating but she is not the only one excluded by the violence of this part of the novel. The chapter describing her should also be read as an indication of the kind of reception that *Hopscotch* gives to Morelli's theories.

If we dismiss Trepat's theories, it is because they have come to us ridiculed by the way in which she has been portrayed as a character. Morelli and Trepat; Carlos Argentino and Borges in "The Aleph": the strategy of presenting a theory and condemning it after attributing it to a despicable character is a frequent device. Trepat's notions of art are dismissed because they have been psychologized to the point of appearing grotesque. Morelli's ideas gain our acceptance more readily, however, because part of their persuasiveness depends on the prestige granted to his relative spareness as a character; we know very little about him. We are mostly given his thoughts, not the details of his daily existence.

Morelli and Trepat together give meaning to this moment in *Hopscotch.* Trepat's failure reveals the powerful hooks of naturalistic discourse; Horacio's humiliation extends much further than the consequences of whatever rumors Trepat wants to spread about him in the neighborhood. This chapter is, more important, a way of framing Morelli and recuperating him for the anecdotal, so that if only for a moment, the vision of the privileged third eye he proposed as an epistemology for his new sense of writing might be obliterated.

Such are the zigzags and false resolutions in *Hopscotch,* consequences of its desire to embrace everything and leave it in suspension; the Morelli-Trepat couple creates the choreography for reading *Hopscotch* against the grain, affirming what the manifesto aspect of the novel seems to want to destroy.

How Should We Read?

The fear of being left outside history, in the margins of experience, being nothing but frivolous consumers, permeates *Hopscotch* and grants energy to the prescriptive moments in the novel as well as to its spirit of denunciation. An ethics of the reader is developed throughout its pages, suggesting that there should be a way of taking the leap that separates those capable of entering the new realm from the dilettantes. Part of this desire is expressed eloquently in Chapter 99:

> In what you've just read to us, it's quite clear that Morelli is condemning in language the reflection of a false or incomplete optic and *Organum* that mask reality and humanity for us. Basically, he didn't really care too much about language, except on the aesthetic plane. But that reference to the ethos is unmistakable. Morelli understands that the mere writing of aesthetic is a fraud and a lie that ends up arousing the female-reader, the type that doesn't want any problems but rather solutions, or false and alien problems that will allow him to suffer comfortably seated in his chair, without compromising himself in the drama that should also be his. In Argentina, if the Club will give me permission to fall back on localisms, that kind of fraud has kept us quite content and peaceful for a whole century. (pp. 359–60)

The mistakenly involved reader, the female reader, and, by extension the Argentine mode of reading, are expelled from the book in this fragment. These pages search for a different kind of reader, not necessarily the one envisioned years earlier by Cortázar's much-admired Macedonio Fernández as the *fantastic reader*, but another one, with amplified tasks. Yet the perspective still remains the same as Macedonio's: literature changes according to its readers who are in charge of effectively realizing it.

Hopscotch attempts to encapsulate all the elements that contribute to its own existence. In shaping its characters as uncomfortable with their conclusions, constantly questioning the meaning of what they say and receive, it suggests one of the possible avenues for reading per se.

The humorous interplay of epigraphs at the beginning of the novel—the first one attributed to the Abad Martini, who alludes to the fruitful results that the young may obtain from reading maxims, counsels, and precepts, and the second attributed to César Bruto, whose games against the rules of Spanish spelling make what he writes sound hilarious—seem to be presented in order to dismantle any pedagogical intentions.[9] Nevertheless, *Hopscotch* does not stop trying to wake up its readers and to beckon them to project themselves into the book, imitating the way in which its characters relate to cultural events and objects.

Thus antipsychologization turns into its opposite because the intellectual characters in the novel take on a mimetic function, this time not in relationship to the world outside the novel but in relationship to the readers of the novel. The message of *Hopscotch* is clear in this respect: the readers' options are enumerated, discarded, and selected by the characters who, in absorbing the readers into the narrative, show them their own faces. A pedagogical task emerges this way, as an attempt to close the circle of interpretation through the establishment of a bridge capable of shattering mirrors.

How should we read? Without reading. We should believe that the book is not there. We should forget about Morelli and Trepat's dance. We should read without sitting in a comfortable armchair. *Hopscotch* is an implacable critic of its own architecture; it tells us not to read literature, perhaps not to even read the book where it says so.

The Naive Reception

There are metaphysical rivers, she swims in them like that swallow swimming in the air, spinning madly around a belfry, letting herself drop so that she can rise all the better with the swoop. I describe and define and desire those rivers but she swims in them. I look for them, find them, observe them from the bridge, but she swims in them. And she doesn't know it, anymore than the swallow. It's not necessary to know things as I do, one can live in disorder, without being held by any sense of order.... La Maga doesn't know who Spinoza is, La Maga reads tedious Russian and German novels and Pérez Galdós and forgets immediately after what she has read. (p. 86)

Being able to forget what one reads amounts to having solved the enigma of the pages and abandon the book without any pending issues. *Hopscotch*'s La Maga is not consumed by the novels she consumes and, even as she is described as Horacio's privileged love quest, she is the embodiment of the female reader. The pleasure she experiences in reading novels while being able to detach herself from their world implies the kind of self-awareness that allows her to put aside what she reads without abandoning herself. The other characters, instead, defined by the opinions they hold about art, literature, and politics, are inextricably linked to those judgments.

La Maga exists on the properly "novelistic" level of representation in *Hopscotch*. Rather than being viewed as a reader, she is perceived as someone to be read. She is the character who is observed, pursued, and desired through the novel, and through her the privileged Surrealistic encounters are made possible. La Maga officiates in the ceremonial level of the book that enables it to be received as plot; both characters and readers are interested in her nature and destiny. Even as La Maga's tastes in reading are punished in the novel, she is herself portrayed as the unknown to be represented.

La Maga loves her son, Rocamadour, but she is a bad mother. Rocamadour's sickness and death are described in one of the most emotionally charged moments of *Hopscotch*; La Maga's fate leaves the other characters speechless as she, part of an anachronistic aesthetic in Morelli's view, captures everybody's attention.

Words in a Mirror

In chapter 32, La Maga writes a letter to Rocamadour, not knowing that he has already died. The chapter begins directly with her words, without any introduction: "Baby, Rocamadour, baby, baby, Rocamadour. By now I know you are like a mirror" (p. 163). La Maga and Rocamadour have a bond that makes their peculiar form of silence possible. La Maga may not know that her son is dead, but even if he were alive, he would not know how to read the letter. She is writing on a mirror—with a finger wet from her tears—that is fogged up by the vapor from a boiling pot of borscht. La Maga's letter is, from its inception, the opposite of a page in a book.

The letter is not there to be preserved, to occupy its own place; the words written literally on the water will disappear. This provisional message to Rocamadour is also anachronistic and mistaken. As a dead addressee, he will not recieve it; were he alive, he would not be able to understand it.

La Maga writes fully aware of the futility of the exercise. Why does she do it then? Who is the true addressee of her words? The reader of *Hopscotch* has replaced Rocamadour and, in that position, reads what La Maga has written. Thus the message changes even though the words remain the same, because the recipient has changed. When La Maga apologizes to Rocamadour for not having gone to visit him, it is the reader who receives La Maga's confession:

> Horacio is right, sometimes I don't care about you at all, and I think you'll thank me for that some day when you'll be able to understand, when you'll be able to see that the best thing was that I'm the way I am. But just the same I cry, Rocamadour, and I write this letter to you because I don't know, because maybe I'm wrong, because maybe I am wicked or sick or a little stupid, not much, just a little, but that's terrible, it makes me sick to my stomach just thinking about it. (p. 166)

Through the letter, La Maga answers the reader's questions about her; the evanescent nature of the medium she has chosen for writing is part of her response. Her intentions, life, and motivations have been inscribed in such a way that they are easily erasable; La Maga writes so that her very being might be aptly forgotten.

La Maga, a reader of long novels she herself forgets immediately after completion, invites us to imitate her: let us follow her in her walks, let us weigh her sentimentalism and maternal capacities, but let us be aware that the explanations we come up with are part of a rapidly disappearing legacy. The anxious pace of our reading, the concentration on her actions—everything evaporates like the words in the mirror. The mirror is left to stand alone, holding the virtuality of a message.

Perishable, too linked to the avatars of one specific book, the reception of La Maga by a first reading of *Hopscotch* relegates her to the role of showing the uncritical, naive position about literature in relationship to the more intelligent and active reading demanded by the novel.

What do we read now in *Hopscotch*? Which among the many representations triggered by following the table of instructions best suits our sense of the contemporary? Once its pedagogical task was completed—to free readers from the somniferous effects of naturalism and realism and rescue them from academic pompousness, preparing them for taking the leap against genre distinctions for a new epistemology—*Hopscotch* elicits other meanings.

Morelli's deliberate theories, the conversations of Horacio and his friends, the constantly parenthetical relationship between thought and act, may now be relegated to a museum of avant-garde artifacts. They are part of a recognizable machinery that has lost its capacity to surprise due to its proliferation in fiction and other domains, such as the paraphilosophical formulations of deconstructionists and poststructuralists.

Thus silenced, that aspect of *Hopscotch* makes another reading of its pages possible. In that alternative reading, we privilege Horacio's walks in the city, the depictions of the streets, the intense physiology of thought as being the live activity taking place in a café or at late night gatherings in small Parisian walk-up apartments, the lovemaking and music, the exile's accents, the foreign words constantly used to evoke a face, Valentin's foot during Berthe Trepat's concert, her breath in the metro, the cold and humidity in winter, the construction of a *here* and *there* by words with aging meanings but still capable of evoking the voices that say them: the creation, in short, of *characters*.[10]

Is this other reading a betrayal? Are we asking the book to accept something that it wanted to punish in its pages? Such issues are the paradoxical results of time and reinterpretation; *Hopscotch* remains alive because of the presence of its characters inscribed in La Maga's mirror.

What About Theory?

Morelli is not the only author whose tutelage is invoked in the novel. César Bruto, an Argentine humorist, who played with misspelling Spanish so that readers might perceive whatever story he told as a joke, provides one of the epigraphs for the novel. His contribution, quoted as being from a work titled *What I Would Like to Be If I Wasn't What I Am* (chapter: "A St. Bernard's Dog") ends as follows: "I jes hope what I been writin down hear do somebody some good so he take a good look at how he livin and he dont be sorry when it too late and everythin is gone down the drain cause it his own fault" (p. 10).

Hopscotch follows the advice of its double meaning: it does take a good look at itself and it also uses the spelling tips to ameliorate the possible pompous effects of subjects discussed with words too grandiose to be taken seriously. The clearest example of the results of César Bruto's lesson occurs in chapter 90, as we observe Horacio at work.

> Oliveira would grab a sheet of paper and write down the grand words over which he went slipping along in his ruminations. He wrote, for example, "The great whaffair," or "the whintersection." It was enough to make him laugh and feel more up to preparing another mate. "Whunity," whrote Wholiveira. "The whego and the whother." He used this *wh* the way other people use penicillin. (p. 341)

Horacio tries to save himself through humor from the solemnity of his own thoughts. The table of instructions in *Hopscotch* attempts to give us a reading pace that would allow us also to hop out from grandiosity into the intensity of true play. Morelli does not use *wh*; his recommendations are locked into a discourse that, because of its earnestness and tendency toward the prescriptive, cannot survive the devastating rewriting of mistaken spelling.

Bad spelling uncovers what is written as style; it takes away its truth and shows it as the result of still another system of conventions. With Morelli gone, César Bruto enters and shows us theory as a joke; our laughter is a celebration of a new paradoxical theoretical framework created by humor and readiness for change.

Risks

In *62: A Model Kit*,[11] a novel that alludes directly to Morelli's efforts, Cortázar writes about a little girl who shows an unspeakable object to her mother. It is something she has seen jump out of the insides of a doll when she accidentally dropped it on the ground. The event leads to the trial and incarceration of M. Ochs, the dollmaker.

M. Ochs is a curious character; his task is the manufacturing of real events through the sudden discovery of secrets he hides inside the dolls. The breaking of the dolls initiates a chain of conflicts, implicating characters into each other's lives. M. Ochs practices a capricious kind of poetry whose elements are the unsuspecting owners of the toys, in this case a little girl and her traumatizing mother.

Two of the novel's main characters, Juan and Tell, talk about the little girl's reaction to the events, stressing a division present in most of Cortázar's work: that between mainstream characters and the loose group of bohemians for whom the world is an adventurous playground:

> "Do you think the girl realized what she had in her hand?" Tell asked. "Not in the least, the poor angel," Juan said, "but her mother's carrying-on must have traumatized her for the rest of her life. When I met Monsieur Ochs I realized that he was much too subtle to waste his time on innocent children; his shots aimed higher, or, as Roger would have put it, he fired three-stage rockets. The first stage was ignited when the girl broke the doll, and, let it be said in passing, she had made good sadistic use of it; the second, which did interest Monsieur Ochs, was the effect the girl's revelations produced on her mother and other members of the family; the third, which placed the capsule in orbit, was the accusation made to the police and the public scandal, which was duly exploited by the press." (p. 101)

M. Ochs is cast here as being healthily subversive in Cortázar's terms; the politics of his objects serve the purpose of illuminating already existent links among the characters and absolve him of any guilt by placing the blame on the conventional mother.

The broken doll breaks the trust that the little girl had in the world. As French girl and mother are thrust into situations they do not quite understand or control, *62: A Model Kit* encourages the reader to laugh by siding with Juan and Tell. Juan and Tell are exiles, and through them Cortázar again makes the point found in *Hopscotch*: that there is a liberating force in foreignness, that the very situation of not belonging to a society facilitates a privileged view of its nature.

The optimism of the early Surrealists is prevalent in the initial reactions to the broken doll as the characters become separated into the conservative-naive (the natives in their own country, exemplified by the mother and daughter), and the free-floating foreigners with an eye to what really matters. M. Ochs is not, however, merely an example of the triumph over the spirit of seriousness so derided by André Breton, Paul Eluard, and others.[12] As Juan finishes telling about the strategies involved in M. Ochs's game with the dolls, his mind starts to wander:

> Tell wanted to know how the episode ended, but Juan had become distracted, thinking about the lotteries of Heliogabalus, about how other girls who opened the bellies of their dolls had found a used toothbrush or a left-handed glove or a thousand-franc note, because many times Monsieur Ochs had put a thousand francs in his dolls, which were scarcely worth five hundred, and someone testified to it at the trial and it was one of the more spectacular of extenuating circumstances, as befits a capitalist society. (p. 101)

The trial ends well for M. Ochs. He is given a modest fine and let out of jail after having thoroughly enjoyed his stay there because of the company of a particularly interesting cellmate, "a specialist in tierce and the topological theories of labyrinths" (p. 102).

Thus M. Ochs's sentence becomes a pretext for the celebration of his capacity for generating surprises through his toys. He has allowed the intervention of chance in the girls' lives. It would be wrong, though, to think that he alone is at issue in the trial. The mothers are also being judged:

> ... but the best result of the trial, and on that Juan and Polanco were in enthusiastic agreement, was that in all of France, a country known for the almost superstitious respect it has for the most useless objects, hordes of disheveled mothers were probably using tongs and shears to open the bellies of their daughters' dolls, in spite of the shrieks of horror from the girls, and not because of any understandable goal of Christian morality, but because the story of the thousand-franc notes had been duly exploited by the afternoon papers that those mothers read. Monsieur Ochs' eyes grew tender as he evoked the shrieks of hundreds of girls who were brutally deprived of their dolls. (p. 102)

As M. Ochs leaves prison we put the mothers on trial. Through the dolls, the rapaciousness of mothers is shown to be an obstacle to play and risk; the mothers are condemned by the reader because of their wish for real currency. As they frighten the little girls, the dolls become an effective currency that unites the girls and M. Ochs in an economy of exchanges destined to exclude the mothers.

These are mothers who, unlike the Uruguayan-born and Parisian exile La Maga from *Hopscotch,* use their desire against their children. Mothers' violence and little girls' fears are played out for the benefit of M. Ochs who, through his dolls, has created a conflict with female puppets in a manner loosely evocative of Morelli. The female theater of motherhood in *62: A Model Kit* presents us with avaricious, violent, and conservative females seen through a detached, philosophical, male eye.

The image of the broken doll is not only a means to unfold what is implicit in mother-daughter realtionships. Tell, one of the characters extremely interested in M. Ochs and his dolls, sends a package containing a doll to Hélène, a much-valued female character in the novel, who is sought after by Juan.

> ... Juan was there in the darkness, that a slow incomprehensible ceremony had brought us closer together in the night of our infinite distances, from Juan's sadness, from your coltish joy, from my hands full of salt, but maybe not, maybe there wasn't any salt left between my fingers, maybe I'd saved myself without knowing it, from a whim of Tell's, from the doll that is Tell and is Juan

and above all is you, and then it would be possible to sleep the way you're sleeping, the way the doll is sleeping in the bed you made for it and wake up closer to you and to Juan and to the world, in a beginning of reconciliation or forgetting, accepting the fact that milk can be spilled on the stove without great to-do, that dishes can stay dirty until nighttime, that a person can live with an unmade bed or with a man who leaves his clothes all over and empties his pipe into the coffee cup. Oh, but then that boy wouldn't have had to die this afternoon. (p. 182)

At this point in the novel, the doll is seen as a link of indisputable materiality among shifting identities. The boy who died is included in the last part of the novel as a burdensome absence, standing in as lover for an "original" of Juan.

What is "the doll that is Tell and is Juan and above all is you"? At one level the "you" designates a character within fiction, the one who made the bed for the doll and is also sleeping in it; the "you" represents, as well, a pressure for readers to find a place for themselves in the doll's economy by making sense of the situation: "tell me that it hasn't been completely useless for Tell to have sent me that doll and that you're there in spite of an unacceptable death under white lights" (p. 183). Thus the doll becomes a tabula rasa for the "you" to be inscribed. It is a "you" that urges the reader to understand someone's death. The one addressing this "you" as she tries to counteract death is Hélène. The scene is reminiscent of La Maga's letter to Rocamadour in *Hopscotch*; there the reader knows that Rocamadour will not have access to the letter, here we read words from somebody, who, looking over Hélène's shoulder, makes us aware of the futility of her hopes:

No Hélène, be true to yourself, my child. There's no way out, the illusion that this hunger for life given you by a girl and her doll can change anything, the signs are clear. Someone dies first, life and the dolls come uselessly afterward. (p. 183)

The voice speaking to Hélène is impersonal and is faithful to Morelli's project in Chapter 62 of *Hopscotch*. It controls her from a higher plane in which she becomes a player in a game she does not quite grasp. The fact that Hélène remains ignorant of the nature of the doll's relationship to death does not turn her into a naive, innocent character. On the contrary, she is capable of inflicting pain. Very much like the little girl in the initial pages of the novel who is frightened by the object inside the doll and by her own mother's reaction, after having satisfied what are referred to as her "sadistic" tendencies toward the doll, Hélène can use the doll as a weapon. In a scene charged with violence, Juan asks Hélène why she has not destroyed the doll completely, since it pains him to know of its existence now as a maimed object. The description of the doll's situation in the room is testimony to the carnality she acquires in the texts and to the affinities that Cortázar's novel has, in this regard, with the work of Hans Bellmer:[13]

> Juan went to the closet and pulled it open. The doll was sitting against the back in the shadows, naked, smiling, in the midst of sheets and towels. Beside it was the box with the clothes, the shoes and a hood; it smelled of sandalwood and maybe burlap. In the half-darkness it was hard to see the break, half hidden by the raised knees. Juan put out his hand and drew the doll out to the lighted part by the edge of the cabinet, where a carefully folded sheet became, on the scale of the doll, a stretcher or an operating table. The body opened up in two on the sheet and Juan saw that Hélène had not even tried to close the break with a piece of adhesive tape, to seal up once more what was lightly pouring out onto the sheet. (pp. 242–43)

The body of the doll is not merely broken, it is *wounded*. Hélène could have destroyed it, she could have done away with the partiality of the doll, but she chose instead to offer it again to Juan and with the wound double the pain that its sight inflicts on him. The body of the doll is an instrument for Hélène to exercise violence on Juan. A woman plays with a doll in order to hurt somebody perceived as being vulnerable. Hélène does not know how to play properly with the doll, since the logic of *62: A Model Kit* owes to Morelli the portrayal of her lack of awareness.

The nonlinear narrative of the novel is complemented by a practice of secrecy creating the illusion that there is always something more behind what is being read. If the doll is an emblem of the kind of objects dreamt up by Morelli, M. Ochs is the archetypical practitioner of the art Morelli foresaw. The naturalistic way in which the doll is presented, the "hordes" of mothers avidly searching inside the bellies of their daughters' toys in a sinister obstetrical parody, and the intensity of Juan's reaction after realizing the state in which Hélène kept her doll, suggest that Morelli's project has resulted in a measure of conventionality that takes it "back" to the contradictions left unresolved in *Hopscotch*. For if Morelli searched for an almost selfless art in which characters would become completely interchangeable, *62: A Model Kit* realizes his project in the form of a novel where gender difference remains within the framework already present in *Hopscotch*.

The sight of Hélène's doll is also the representation of women inflicting pain and fear. The "primal" scene of the novel begin the lightness of an evocation of petty, mainstream French mothers as seen by unsympathetic foreigners, but soon the light humor gives way to the ruthlessness of the women handling the dolls.

The mothers may inflict pain on their daughters precisely because of their essential link to them; Hélène may hurt Juan because of his passion for her. These women use the passions they evoke to instill fear and pain. We have now guessed the doll's secret: it is the imminence of being wounded by female love.

The dolls' broken bodies circulate, making toys of their users. Inevitably, it is men who laugh (at the mothers or the girls in the original scenes) or are hurt. Laughter or pain, the fear of the female body whose belly opens up to show the unspeakable, is the dark undertaking of *62: A Model Kit.*

The realization of Morelli's project remains a virtuality, the traps of identity he had hoped to write off remain in this novel, with the dolls recreating a world neatly separated into two genders.

An Abyss

In *62: A Model Kit* the dolls speak the language of the silent horror of her opened belly. The novel is traversed by the suspicion that stories of blood and death underlie everyday reality, a suggestion mediated by the presence of the Countess Erzsébet Bathory, whose murderous exploits are evoked throughout the text.[14] The Countess provides a historical counterpoint to the narrative, showing that the horror elicited by a doll that may be imaginary was concretely executed by one of the most notable murderers in history.

Cortázar's short stories, obsessed by the relationship between everyday reality and the uncanny, often delve into the issues we have uncovered.

In "Press Clippings," a story from the collection *We Love Glenda So Much,*[15] we read a narrative that uses newspaper clippings detailing a crime in Marseilles and documents about tortures and disappearances that took place during the late 1970s in Argentina. The use of such materials interested Cortázar, who always sought ways to fit disparate pieces of the "real" world into his writing. His novel *Libro de Manuel* is a testimony to the most sustained effort he made in his regard, although it is not as successful as "Press Clippings," which manages to encapsulate in a much shorter and persuasive form that which already existed in *Libro de Manuel* as a weakly executed project.

"Press Clippings" tells us from the outset that the clipping about the crime in Marseilles, allegedly taken from the French newspaper *France Soir,* is invented, whereas all the others are not. As in *Libro de Manuel,* the clippings are exchanged by characters who are foreigners living in Paris and are removed from the events mentioned in the clippings.

The characters are Noemí, a writer in whose voice the story is told, and an unnamed sculptor who asks her to write a text about his work.

I was glad that there wasn't anything systematic or too explicative in the sculptor's work, that each piece had something of an enigma about it and that sometimes one had to look for a long time in order to understand the modality that violence assumed there; the sculptures seemed to me to be at the same time naive and subtle, in any case, without any sense of dread or sentimental exaggeration. (p. 82)

Noemí and the sculptor discover that they indeed have the affinities needed for her to write about his work and, after reading newspaper clippings about tortures in Argentina, they become exhausted. Noemí says good-bye and goes out at night into the streets, where she encounters a private drama of sex and violence. She meets a little girl who asks her to come with her, only to find herself a participant in a scene of domestic sadism:

His back to me, sitting on a bench, the girl's papa was doing things to her mama; he was taking his time, slowly lifting his cigarette to his mouth, letting the smoke out of his nose slowly while the lighted end came down to rest on one of mama's breasts, remained there for the duration of the gagged shrieks under the towel wrapped around her mouth and face except for the eyes. (p. 91)

Noemí, incapable of just watching, hits the man with a stool and frees the woman. To her shock, the woman starts doing to the man the same things he had done to her. Noemí flees and writes an account of these occurrences as the text she had promised the sculptor.

Noemí's flight, her text, and the confusion between the private drama in Marseilles and the actual Argentine tortures are joined in the narrative by the recollection of a passage from Jack London, in which "a trapper in the north struggles to win a clean death while beside him, turned into a bloody thing that still holds a glimmer of consciousness, his comrade in adventures howls and twists, tortured by the women of the tribe" (p. 93). The story gathers all these elements in such a way that, though separate, they are tightly connected by an inner logic. Through that logic we proceed from one form of violence to another, very much like Mecha, a character in the story "Nightmares" in the same volume, who wakes up from a painful comatose dream only to become part of the Argentine violence of the 1970s.

Noemí does not experience any moral satisfaction in saving the woman from the hands of her man. Together with the sculptor she tries to translate into another medium the violence she sees around her. But her forced participation in the Marseilles crime is an indication of the extent to which detachment is denied her; the translator, then, becomes enmeshed in the articulations of a language that cannot be considered foreign any longer.

"Those who survived were shot that same Christmas night" the sculptor read aloud. "They probably gave them sweet rolls and cider, remember that in Auschwitz they passed out candy to the children before sending them into the gas chambers." He must have seen something in my face, he made a gesture of apology, and I lowered my eyes and looked for another cigarette. (pp. 84–85)

The reference to Auschwitz may be tamed by the sculptor's averting his eyes, but the story tells us that violence does not admit mere observers. It is all-embracing and no one is free from its contamination.

Pleasure in eating and drinking before entering the gas chambers: Cortázar returns time and again to the abysses opened up as we try to make sense of how we live, write, and read. That he also became intertwined in the forms of children's play as they may delineate our desires is testimony to how radical a discovery he foresaw in playing games and forging fictions.

Notes

1. This interview appeared in *Review of Contemporary Fiction* (Fall 1983): 5–25. A longer version of this same interview appeared in Evelyn Picón Garfield's *Cortázar por Cortázar* (Veracruz, Mexico: Universidad Veracruzana, 1978).

2. The reaction of the Cuban writer José Lezama Lima is exemplary: "The novel meditates on the novel; finally words are experiences because words and experiences are inspired by a tragic hilarity. The reader jumps on the writer, new man of Zoar and, together, they make a new centaur. The reader, punished and favored by the gods at the same time, is blinded, but he is granted prophetic vision. The reader is convinced, according to Cortázar, that 'the novel is a coagulant of experiences, a catalyst of confused and misunderstood notions' because the author is convinced that 'only gestational matters' are worthwhile and the reader again, as though inside a quartz polyhedron, acquires the diversity of refraction and obstinacy of a wandering point," *Revista de Casa de las Américas* (Cuba) 7, 49 (July–August 1968): 68; the translation is mine. See also Héctor Schmucler's "*Rayuela*: Juicio a la literatura," *Pasado y Presente* (Córdoba, Argentina) (April–September 1965): 29–45, to gauge the extent to which *Rayuela* was, from the outset, designated as the book that would revolutionize reading.

3. Cortázar is frequently thought of as a follower of Surrealism. Part of his fiction develops a vision that the French Surrealists stated programmatically in literature. The particular weight accorded to words and to the secret logic of their combination as seen by the Surrealists is a matrix for some of Cortázar's efforts. The words used by Pierre Naville referring to the Surrealists certainly applies to the Cortázar of *62, Modelo para armar*: "Mots déhalés, promis au sort incertain d'une *divinatoire* plus encore que d'une combinatoire." See Pierre Naville, *Le temps du surréel*, vol. 1 (Paris: Galilée, 1977), p. 119. Cortázar's play with the humorous possibilities of science when overlapped with punning relates to Benjamin Peret, "Ces animaux de la famille," in the journal *La Révolution surréaliste* (Paris: Gallimard, March 1, 1926): 14–15, republished in

the facsimile edition, *La Révolution surréaliste* (Paris: Jean-Michel Place, 1976). But it is with the vision of the painters of that period that Cortázar may be most accurately compared, haunted as he is by similar concerns with voyeurism and the marriage between sex and death. Compare, for example, the illustration by André Masson for the Marquis de Sade's *Justine* with Cortázar's evocation of looking through the peephole in *62, Modelo para armar*. See André Masson's illustration for *Justine*, reproduced in *Obliques*, nos. 12–13 (Paris: Éditions Borderie, 1977), p. 14.

4. Julio Cortázar, *Rayuela* (Buenos Aires: Editorial Sudamericana, 1963). Citations are in accordance with the English translation by Gregory Rabassa, *Hopscotch* (New York: Avon, 1975).

5. Julio Cortázar, *62, Modelo para armar* (Buenos Aires: Editorial Sudamericana, 1968). Citations are in accordance with the English translation by Gregory Rabassa, *62: A Model Kit* (New York: Random House, 1972). For a further study of this aspect of Cortázar's work, see Ana María Barrenechea, "Horacio en el proceso de escritura de *Rayuela*: Pre-texto y texto," *Sur* 350–51 (1982): 45–63. Saúl Yurkievich explores the energy generated by *Hopscotch* in "La pujanza insumisa," in the critical edition of *Rayuela*, edited by Julio Ortega and Saúl Yurkievich (Madrid: CSIC, 1991), pp. 661–74.

6. *Trepat* in French has connotations of death; Horacio's interaction with Berthe Trepat unfolds the possibilities of her name. The bleakness of Trepat's representation, an almost naturalistic evocation with the sense of immediacy found in descriptions by Céline, is integrated into the novel through a logic of contrasts and chance. "La terreur illumine brutalement l'objet, où le désir, le plaisir et nous parlerons de menace, de charme, de dégoût quand il nous faudra par la suite nous expliquer avec nous mêmes," writes Paul Nouge in "La vision déjouée," originally published in *Le Surréalisme au service de la Révolution* (Paris: Éditions des Cahiers Libres, May 1933): 26, reprinted in *Le Surréalisme au service de la Révolution*.

7. The fear of older women appears often in contemporary Latin American fiction. The most notable examples are in Carlos Fuentes's *Aura* and José Donoso's *The Obscene Bird of Night*. An older woman's desires and aspirations appear in this tradition as intimations of death, ridicule, or witchcraft. Deprived of a desirable body, this kind of woman is made to represent an unspeakable threat. I explore some aspects of this issue in Chapter 8, devoted to Donoso.

8. Both stories appeared in Julio Cortázar, *Final del juego* (Buenos Aires: Sudamericana, 1974). I have studied them in detail in the context of Cortázar's perspective on the uncanny in my *Figuras furiosas* (Paris: Revista Rio de la Plata, 1985), pp. 113–24. See also Alfred J. MacAdam, *El individuo y el otro: Crítica a los cuentos de Julio Cortázar* (Buenos Aires: Librería, 1971), and Saúl Yurkievich, *Julio Cortázar: Al calor de tu sombra* (Buenos Aires: Legasa, 1987).

9. Cortázar uses quotations here in order to contest authority rather than to affirm it. They are elements with a visual as well as intellectual impact on the reader. They recall a context as they redefine it because of their fragmentary nature. The use of the fragment in Cortázar, with its humorous reverberations, may be traced back to his fascination with the work of artists who combined visual and written elements in their work, in particular Marcel Duchamp. A good example may be found in Ecke Bonk, *Marcel Duchamp: The Box in a Valise*, trans. David Britt (New York: Rizzoli, 1989).

10. Jean Andreu studies the traits of Cortázar's characters as they are produced in an interplay with the categories of author and reader. See Jean Andreu, "Personnage, lecteur, auteur," *L'Arc* 80: 24–34.

11. As I indicated in the first chapter of this volume, the organization of *62: A Model Kit* owes much to Macedonio Fernández's *Museum of the Novel of the Eternal*.

12. Cortázar engages in that kind of humorous warfare in *Historias de cronopios y de famas* (Buenos Aires: Ediciones Minotauro, 1962), *La vuelta al día en ochenta mundos* (México: Siglo XXI 1967), *Ultimo Round* (Madrid: Siglo XXI, 1967), and *Los autonautas de la cosmopista* (Barcelona: Muchnik Editores, 1986). His practice, although understandable in terms of Dada and Surrealism, sets the proposals of these schools in a new dimension to the extent that he mainstreams what for the Surrealists was a group-oriented activity in which private complicities were crucial. The Surrealists' affinities with Cortázar's purposes are clear: "In one particular and important respect Surrealist play is more like a kind of provocative magic. This is in its irrepressible propensity to the *transformation* of objects, behavior and ideas. In this aspect of its proceedings Surrealism makes manifest its revolutionary intent," Mel Gooding, ed., *Surrealist Games* (Boston: Shambhala Redstone Editions, 1993), p. 12 (boxed edition containing games).

13. I refer to the *carnality* attained by Bellmer's mangled dolls, a feeling also conveyed in Cortázar's novel. See Sarane Alexandrian, *Hans Bellmer* (New York: Rizzoli, 1972).

14. The Countess Erzsébet Bathory is a legendary murderess born in Hungary. She is said to have killed hundreds of young women in order to drink their blood. Her death, in 1614, after a long criminal trial, turned her into a figure of the perverse stature of Gilles de Rais. The countess is the subject of a book by Valentine Penrose, *La comtesse sanglante* (Paris: Gallimard, 1962). Cortázar's friend the poet Alejandra Pizarnik also wrote about her, inspired, no doubt, by Valentine Penrose.

15. Quotations from "Press Clippings" are in accordance with *We Love Glenda So Much*, trans. Gregory Rabassa (New York: Knopf, 1983).

Chapter 5
A Poetics of Misencounters: Adolfo Bioy Casares

> Sometimes, when I can't do anything but begin a story the way I would like to begin this one, precisely when I would like to be Adolfo Bioy Casares.
> —Julio Cortázar[1]

> I believe I am free of every superstition of modernity, of any illusion that yesterday differs intimately from today or will differ from tomorrow; but I maintain that during no other era have there been novels with such admirable plots as *The Turn of the Screw, Der Prozess, Le Voyageur sur la Terre,* and the one you are about to read, which was written in Buenos Aires by Adolfo Bioy Casares.
> —Jorge Luis Borges[2]

    The first epigraph belongs to Cortázar, who writes about his wish to be Bioy Casares as he starts writing a story that he would like to tell with the kind of detachment and precision he admires in Bioy Casares's work. The quotation from Borges is part of the preface he wrote to *Morel's Invention*. These words, written for the 1940 first edition of the novel, are not only a testimony to the admiration he felt for it but an indication of the literary friendship between Borges and Bioy Casares, which over the years produced a number of texts in collaboration and an intertwining of the works they signed separately. This is explicitly the case, for example, in Borges's "Tlon, Uqbar, Orbis Tertius."[3]
    The story Cortázar wishes he could tell like Bioy Casares is a love entanglement involving the narrator and a woman named Anabel, whose name evokes Edgar Allan Poe and Juan Carlos Onetti.[4] Cortázar locates the problems he encounters in finding out how to go about his writing in a counterpoint between Bioy Casares and Jacques Derrida, whose "La vérité en peinture" he quotes.[5]

Cortázar could not have coupled two more disparate writers than Derrida and Bioy Casares because, although some of the ultimate consequences of their conceptions of literary representation might coincide, the modes of reading they each invite are opposed. Cortázar understands the tension between these two writers and offers the story as a means to understand the particular place in which his own attempts might be located. From Derrida he reproduces some lines about the relationship between subject and object; in Bioy Casares he admires the capacity for detachment, the ease and synthesis of his prose. The story that Cortázar wants to tell concerns a misadventure with Anabel. In that respect, he has been able to reproduce a quality that haunts Bioy Casares's work—endowing the entanglements of love with somber impossibilities, humorous complicities with the reader, and a dangerous imminence of the fantastic.

Of Machines and Writing

In a scene from Erich von Stroheim's memorable film *Foolish Wives*, a Russian nobleman played by von Stroheim looks at the reflection in a mirror of a retarded girl he has selected as a victim. The viewer needs the barest information about what follows; the light and the expression in von Stroheim's face as he looks at her in the mirror are already a rape. The crime has already taken place symbolically in the mirror before it is actually executed.

Before becoming a criminal, the Russian nobleman is an artifice; before being a protagonist in his own experience, he is a spectator who watches the very elements that make up his own representation. In this context it matters little whether the crime is actually committed; the violence of the plot is already in the mirror. The pact between victim and executioner has been sealed, and the viewer knows that any other twist in the plot would only be a violation of the mirror's precise economy.

In *Foolish Wives*, as in other silent movies, the absence of sound grants a nightmarish vividness to the images, a faithfulness to their visual nature that is not as immediate in films with sound. The plot is always inferior to the density of nondiscursive images; the captions in silent film are trivial in relation to the allusive power of the frames. Silent films may be more faithful to the nature of their medium. The Russian nobleman observing his victim is a reduced model of the mirrorings effected by film; he is *seen* and *sees* simultaneously elements that are to be articulated by a spectator projected in a character who is also portrayed as witness.

A vast part of Bioy Casares's work is to be understood in its relationship to the visual as found in film. His relationship to this medium, however, does not involve quotation of films, such as we find in Manuel Puig, for example, but instead grapples with the relationships between the different layers sustaining visual representation and the kind of detachment built into being a spectator.[6]

Morel's Invention suggests one of the ways in which Bioy Casares formulates the issue. The novel is narrated by a man in flight who wants to leave a record of his experiences. He refers to the existence of a museum and to the fact that he is on an island where there are mosquitoes and aquatic plants. The report is written uncomfortably and with great anxiety:

The heat was so intense that after I had been out of the pool for only two or three minutes I was already bathed in perspiration again. As day was breaking, I awoke to the sound of a phonograph record. Afraid to go back to the museum to get my things, I ran away down through the ravine. (p. 9)

There are other people on the island; the narrator is above all obsessed with meeting a woman named Faustine. We learn later that the meeting is impossible because Faustine is an image projected by a machine.

The narrator considers different strategies in his efforts to get closer to Faustine; the sight of her makes him feel inadequate but also incapable of doing anything but try to approach her:

Then, while waiting to speak to her, I was reminded of an old psychological law. It was preferable to address her from a high place that would make her look up to me. The elevation would compensate, at least in part, for my defects. (p. 24)

We are initiated into the protagonist's desire by the awareness of an inequality in love; his embarrassment makes him delay the moment of getting closer to her. Although that closeness remains impossible, given the fact that Faustine is a projected image, the reader is so caught by the rhythm of this deferral of action that when the protagonist does decide to utter some words, they are startling:

"Please, young lady," I said, "will you please listen to me," but I hoped she would not listen, because I was so excited I had forgotten what I was going to say. The words "young lady" sounded ridiculous on the island. And besides my sentence was too imperative (combined with my sudden appearance there, the time of day, the solitude).

I persisted: "I realize you may not wish—" But I find it impossible now to recall exactly what I said. I was almost unconscious. I spoke in a slow, subdued voice with a composure that suggested impropriety. I repeated the words "young lady." (pp. 24–25)

The man embarrassed by his words sliding toward the sleazy pick-up, obscenity, impropriety. The coarseness with which the "young lady" is perceived is a product of the interruption of the protracted silence that, while there, opened up countless possibilities of contact between the characters. Once the silence is broken, the anonymous "young lady" sets limits to the eloquence of the situation. The universality of the island becomes erased; we enter the realm of the concrete, of daily existence. The slippage toward vulgarity, the commonplace, and the familiar are rejected in *Morel's Invention*. Instead, being attracted by another is seen as enjoying the pleasures of detachment, whereas closeness signals the end of the freedom granted by separation.

Faustine's power resides in her capacity for revealing, as an image, the weaknesses of the man who desires her, through his fear that in uttering words that define him he will also show the pettiness of his aspirations. Thus *Morel's Invention* focuses on the parenthetical aspects of love by prolonging the tensions of the misencounter and, in a resolution that echoes E. T. A. Hoffmann's Olympia,[7] it suggests that the loved woman is nothing but a projected image. If the impossibility of contact resides in the radical difference between the characters, the intention of overcoming the distance is portrayed as a somberly heroic gesture.

The fleeing character in *Morel's Invention* attempts to save himself through love and become part of the same system of representation that reproduces the image of Faustine. The novel suggests that such an encounter is not to take place; a kind of nostalgia colors the awareness that it may be mechanically impossible to integrate the protagonist into the film that shows his loved one to him time and again. The music, "Tea for Two" and "Valencia," provides a sentimental background for the film sequences, in contrast to the harsh island existence with its mosquitoes and humidity.

Loving Faustine is equivalent to thinking of oneself as dead, invisible, a puppet:

And I still wonder: what does all this mean? Certainly, she is a detestable person. But what is she after? She may be playing with the bearded man and me; but then again he may be a tool that enables her to tease me. She does not care if she makes him suffer. Perhaps Morel only serves to emphasize her complete repudiation of me, to portend the inevitable climax and the disastrous outcome of this repudiation!

But if not—Oh, it has been such a long time now since she has seen me. I think I shall kill her or go mad, if this continues any longer. I find myself wondering whether the disease-ridden marshes I have been living in have made me invisible. And, if that were the case, it would be an advantage: then I could kidnap Faustine without any danger— (p. 33)

The published English translation renders the last phrase as "then I could *seduce* Faustine without any danger"; the original reads "podría *raptar* a Faustine sin ningún peligro." *Raptar* means to kidnap, an important distinction for *Morel's Invention* because the protagonist carefully avoids any intimation of untoward plans in his desire to join Faustine. The novel stresses a counterpoint in his feelings between total incapacity to rise to the challenge of the woman he desires and the brazen actions he thinks are needed to take her away; seduction has no place here. The narrator considers his condition as invisible outsider through the desire to join Faustine and concludes it is an advantage. Persecuted by his enemies in the "reality" of his adventure and also in the projected images that turn Faustine's companions into his rivals, he builds a problematic bridge toward the reader. The report he writes tries to clarify doubts and give information by forging a bond with the reader that parallels the approach in his earlier novel, *Plan for Escape*.[8]

The reader is granted the invisibility that the protagonist wants for himself; unseen by the characters in the novel, the reader look at the protagonist looking at Faustine while also trying to explain what he or she sees as he listens in the mind to "Tea for Two" and "Valencia":

> Here is some evidence that can help my readers establish the date of the intruders' second appearance here: the following day two moons and two suns were visible. . . . I am not mentioning them because of any poetic attachment, or because of their rarity, but rather to give my readers, who receive newspapers and celebrate birthdays, a way to date these pages. (p. 45)

Unlike Faustine, the narrator wants to be the reader's friend. But is he really helping the reader to frame what the report says? Is *Morel's Invention* positing behind the disjointed couple of Faustine and the narrator an ideal couple consisting of reader and narrator? The reader cannot date the pages, despite being subjected to such chronological data as birthdays; the excess of information provided disconcerts the reader as much as it does the protagonist. Thus the appeals to direct dialogue with a hypothetical reader delineate the image of another character, the narrator's double, who relates to the text with the same kind of difficulty that the narrator has as he goes through his adventure.

The main role of the protagonist of *Morel's Invention* is to be a witness. His experience consists of observing and trying to interpret what he sees as he strives to discover the mechanism of the machine producing the images he observes. His report is the very purpose of his adventure; his text is an attempt to reproduce the images he sees already reproduced:

Chapter 5

If one day the images should fail, it would be wrong to suppose that I have destroyed them by writing this diary. . . . A recluse can make machines or invest his visions with reality only imperfectly, by writing about them or depicting them to others who are more fortunate than he. (p. 70)

Morel's Invention registers the inexorable loss of the immediacy of its images. Only copies survive, with markings of the fissures that separate them from their originals; the narrator is the discoverer of those fissures and, at the same time, the producer of additional ones through the writing of his report, that other machine of representations.

Morel's Invention is a violent novel. Its machine of representation cancels the references that support it; its articulation of the visual consists of undermining the reliability of the projected images, and the clues given throughout the text are only there to be obliterated by interpretation.

The narrator-reader couple is constituted here in oblique celebration of its disjunction subject to the virtuality of their link in a paralyzing and repetitive logic. Faustine remains floating, shifting names and gender, silent, and remote in a multiplicity of representations. It is no doubt this aspect of *Morel's Invention* that prompted Borges to claim for it the lineage of Louis Auguste Blanqui and Dante Gabriel Rossetti.

Bioy Casares continued to pose the puzzling questions introduced here in other works; his short fantastic stories frequently engage the figure of repetition. "The Celestial Plot"[9] has the most affinities with *Morel's Invention*. The name of Blanqui appears there explicitly to render more credible the experience of a protagonist who, sick and disconcerted, is lost in parallel and barely connected worlds. Blanqui, who spent time in prison himself, was forbidden to look at the outside world from the window of a cell near the sea. He formulated eloquently the despair caused by the kind of infinity produced by endless repetition in his book *L'eternité par les astres*:[10]

What we call progress is bolted into each planet earth, and fades with it. Always and everywhere in the terrestrial sphere, the same drama, the same backdrop and the same narrow stage, a noisy humanity, infatuated with its greatness believing itself the universe and living in its prison as in an immensity, to succumb in short order along with the globe which has borne in the greatest disdain the burden of its pride. The same monotony, the same immobility, in the alien stars. The universe repeats itself endlessly and prances about in place. Imperturbably, eternity plays out the same performance through infinity." (p. 169)

Morel's Invention tells us that love, writing, and watching projected images circulate in parallel worlds that turn those who try to grasp them into proliferating versions of themselves.

Streets and Commonplaces

The embarrassment associated with the idea of approaching Faustine and the uncomfortable relationship with the use of commonplaces are not to be found in later works by Bioy Casares, where, on the contrary, he delves into clichés, local references, and the feel of the city of Buenos Aires. The change that shifts his language toward the colloquial involves a way of conceiving the bonds of love. The novel *Asleep in the Sun*[11] explores, like *Morel's Invention*, the relationship between characters and their supposedly "original" selves.

The novel is divided in two sections: one that occupies most of the book, said to be by Lucio Bordenave, and a shorter one, by Félix Ramos. Félix Ramos is the reader's twin because Bordenave writes the report so that he can read it and be persuaded of his adventure. By acknowledging the text, Ramos grants it existence. His testimony as a reader is qualified by the fact that he is part of the same fictional web as Bordenave, but because he is the point of departure for Bordenave's account and the closing voice of the novel, he stands for the hypothetical reader of any novel. Thus reader and writer have metamorphosed into Bordenave and Ramos. Bordenave is an unreliable author who writes from a sanitarium and Ramos is a critic of his text, victim of the inevitable complicity entailed by being part of the intrigues that brought him there.

Bordenave suffers from an amorous obsession. He wants to know what he loves about his wife, Diana, her body or her soul. His sense of Diana is fragmented but detailed: "I am mad about her shape and her size, her rosy complexion, her blond hair, her delicate hands, her smell, and, above all, her incomparable eyes" (p. 16). Since Diana is not an indivisible unity (she may be fragmented as a smell, a hair color, the shape of her hands) the suspicion arises that her parts may be rearranged into a different system. The novel expands this possibility by presenting us with an institution called Sanatorio Frenopático, where a special kind of surgery is performed. Physical parts and souls belonging to humans and to dogs are exchanged in a hyperbolic rendition of what is merely suggested in Bordenave's account of how Diana sits on her chair: "cuddled up in a armchair, hugging one leg, with her face resting on a knee, gazing into empty space" (p. 16).

After careful analysis souls and bodies are separated. Once the surgery is performed the issue is determining whether those who emerge from the hospital are the same as when they went in, that is, whether there is between them and their names that kind of continuity that allows for recognition.

Diana has two doubles: Adriana María, her sister, and a dog who has the soul that they took out of Adriana Mariá in the Frenopático. Sister and dog have resemblances and differences in relationship to Diana. Her sister has a different color hair but Bordenave emphasizes that otherwise they are the same; the dog has her soul and occasionally Bordenave suggests that this is what he loves best in her.

Diana has somebody's (the dog's?) healthy soul; she is a healed patient who comes out of the hospital. Bordenave alternatively describes her in his account as having been cured or as having turned into someone else. Diana is herself to the extent that she responds to her name and has the same body she had before the operation. Her sister is also Diana since they have almost identical bodies. The dog is Diana because she has its soul. According to the criteria of the Frenopático, Bordenave is not completely sane; furthermore, his account reaches us as it is written to an old enemy, Félix Ramos. Bordenave speaks in a paranoid and agitated manner at the end of the novel and suggests the possibility of having been betrayed by the ever elusive Diana.

Ramos, who had himself been institutionalized in the Frenopático in the past, shows himself to be a questionable witness as he attempts to give us testimony to better our understanding of Bordenave's adventure:

> I don't have faith in the document's authenticity. First of all, it seems strange that Bordenave would write to me; after all, we've parted ways. It also seems strange that Bordenave addresses me in a formal manner; after all, we've known each other since childhood. (p. 188)

Félix Ramos's testimony is suspect because of the extent of his involvement with Bordenave. The closing words of the novel—Ramos's statement that "the whole matter seemed, apart from confusing, threatening. So I decided to forget about it for a while" (p. 190)—bring Ramos and Bordenave together by indicating the possibility of a future detailed investigation by Ramos (similar to Bordenave's about Diana) that would have the same consequences it had for Bordenave: land him again in the Frenopático as a patient.

Bordenave has addressed his account to an enemy, who is also his double, and who, on reading it, translates Bordenave's destiny into his own. The exchanges between Bordenave and Ramos are governed, in a less explicit interplay, by the same logic as the transplants of bodies and souls. The novel is the machinery of transplants in the Frenopático; its title highlights words by the doctor:

> "I imagine a dog, sleeping in the sun, in a raft that floats slowly downstream, on a wide, calm stream."
> —"And then?"

—"Then"—he answered—"I imagine I am that dog and I fall asleep." (p. 174)

Falling asleep is substituting one sleeper for another in a kind of self-awareness that is also self-destruction. The hypothesis of the body and soul transplantation questions whatever might be perceived as essential in one's personal identity. *Asleep in the Sun* confuses Bordenave with Ramos, multiplies Diana, and, instead of a linear plot, offers us a web of interconnections, a *trama*.

As in *Morel's Invention*, *Asleep in the Sun* tends to present its own conditions of representation, but unlike *Morel's Invention* the uncanny effects of narration are carried out in everyday language, quite distinct from the austerity found in the earlier novel. Nevertheless, the proximity that Bordenave wants to achieve to Diana is as unattainable as that sought by the protagonist of *Morel's Invention* with Faustine.

Diana, who is more vulgar than Faustine, neurotic, with lower class manners, surrounded by characters of humble social extraction, and unlike those film aristocrats who are referred to in *Morel's Invention* as "the heroes of snobbishness or the inhabitants of an abandoned mental hospital," is also beyond reach. The desire to possess her puts the identity of the pursuer in danger as it disassembles the desired object into irreconcilable parts, body and soul, which have forever lost their harmony. Like the mythological Diana, but in a domesticated and porteño version, knowing about her destroys him who wants to observe her. The married couple in *Asleep in the Sun* is a familiar and parodic rewriting of the figures of detachment that *Morel's Invention* offers in a more desperate and austere register.

Dr. Samaniego, a direct reference to the author of the fables, has been able to perform his task admirably. Animals do speak with human voices. But is there a moral to this fable? What lesson is to be drawn from these characters, who proceed from betrayal to suspicion to humiliation, all the while suggesting their shared nature with dogs? For an answer to these questions we must turn to still another machine of representation, this time a camera.

The Flight

Morel's Invention conjectures that a man ought to speak to a woman from a higher position in order to conquer her attention and avoid ridicule; *Asleep in the Sun* suggests that she ought to be spied on, subjected to surgery, and married, while recognizing that even so she remains elusive. *A Photographer's Adventure in La Plata*[12] further explores these problems and gives them another twist through the presentation of a gallery of female characters.

In this novel it is the women who pursue a man, Nicolasito Almanza, a photographer from Buenos Aires who goes to the city of La Plata on a photo assignment. During his first walk in La Plata Nicolasito meets a family, the Lombardos, whose way of positioning themselves makes him think that they are posing for a group photograph. As he grows closer to the members of the family, the feeling that they are being held together by some kind of unstated bond that makes Nicolasito an outsider is emphasized.

As is common in La Plata, a city with a major university and populated by numerous students, Nicolasito is lodged in a boarding house. Carmen, the landlady, has a rule ostensibly set to maintain the morals of the place: she does not allow the boarders to invite women to their rooms. Nicolasito's friend, Mascardi, is a simple-minded fellow who tries to show Nicolasito the positive side of the rule when he sees him with a forlorn expression on his face:

—"What's the matter, you seem, I don't know, down, sad. Don't tell me that the landlady's lecture depressed you."
—"And why should I be depressed?"
"Because women are not allowed in here. Want to know what I think? For people such as ourselves, it's a plus. The unavoidable woman who is too much doesn't bother us. One gets into the boarding house and is safe. Outside, we have the Mascardi organization."
There was no way out but to ask what it was. Mascardi explained that he knew some students who had an apartment. In La Plata there were groups of five or six per apartment. As a general rule, once a week they were visited by a woman. . . .
Mascardi added that there were also women who offered themselves on the sidewalk, screaming their hearts out, as the Chilean students say.
Looking at him with an expressionless face, Almanza commented:
—"The truth is you've become a womanizer." (p. 29)

Almanza's lack of enthusiasm about the shelter provided by the boarding house and the possible thrill of future sexual encounters is in part due to his having given blood a short while earlier for a transfusion to help the father of the Lombardo family, in an episode rife with intimations of vampirism and manipulation.

The women in *A Photographer's Adventure in La Plata* act differently from Faustine and Diana. They offer themselves in body and image to the photographer. The disagreeable Carmen lusts for him and spies on him constantly; the women of the family he met by chance in the street pay excessive attention to him and give him their bodies with a remarkable celerity. Nicolasito does not share their intense desire for physical contact; his relationships to women are mediated by the camera lens:

He thought that Julia did not grimace when she cried and that he would like to photograph that pretty face, covered by tears. He told her that she was very pretty.
Julia answered:
—"Then kiss me. (p. 109)

Julia asks Nicolasito to kiss her; the landlady kisses him after he finishes photographing her for a portrait, while he is thinking about how horrible the results will be. Both women, the beautiful one who is the ideal model for an attractive picture and the ugly one, with a triple chin and bags under the eyes, want to move quickly from the photo session to having sexual relations. Almanza lives these liaisons with varying degrees of involvement, acquiescence, or rejection but always with the detachment of a tourist.

Almanza's adventure, rich in presumed dangers and suspicions of a conspiracy by the Lombardo family, brings him into contact with women who are Faustine's opposite; they are too talkative,[13] vulgar, physically aggressive, merely pretty, or decidedly ugly. Like Faustine, though, they are all separated from Nicolasito by a means of representation. We do not have here Morel's machine or the complicated surgeries of the Frenopático; instead, we read about a camera that Nicolasito puts between himself and his models. The camera acts like a shield that separates him from "real" experience to turn him into an agent for representation, safe from the women's emotional excesses. Nicolasito does not choose for himself an elevated place, like the protagonist of *Morel's Invention,* he prefers to be merely *outside,* even as he goes through the motions of living a romance with one of the Lombardo women, Julia.

A Photographer's Adventure in La Plata closes with the suggestion that the dangers faced by Almanza may have been imaginary but were of enough weight for the relationship with Julia to end. The last scene, a sentimental cliché, shows Julia leaving in a bus without there having been any conversation between them about the reasons for the imminent separation or the meaning of their attachment.

They announced the departures for Balcarce, Tandil, and Azul.
—"You should get in."
She obeyed. Knocking at the glass, because he could not open, he started yelling to her:
—"I wanted to tell you. . . ."
Julia was covering her face so that he would not see her cry and she was saying something to him he could not hear. (p. 223)

The reader, in a photographer's position, perceives this scene (with its echoes of such films as *Casablanca* and so many others picturing separation and broken romance) already framed with its sentimental charge but so filtered by the clarity of the allusions that a humorous current surfaces.

Separated by a glass that echoes the novel's numerous references to windows, crystals, kaleidoscopes, and stained glass, the characters are refracted and show us the truth of their separation, the unheard words, in a silence that stands as final definition of the chatter that had joined them. Each of them remains with a different story about this story— the women who ask for a kiss, the photographer who gives it but thinks about his photographs—each of them separate but still linked to the other by the illusion that somehow they may surmount the distance between them.

In another story by Bioy Casares, "The Women's Hero," two characters attempt to remember a film and wonder about its end:

> —"With whom did the female star end up?"—asked Laura.
> —"Whom would she end up with?" replied don Nicolas—"with the hero."
> —"The women's hero"—observed Laura—"is not always the men's hero."
> —"A great truth; but don't forget my lady, that in the movies there is only one hero." (p. 161)

Bioy Casares's literature reveals that the hero's women are many but that they are all the same underneath their differences. Whether portrayed as exasperating, delicate, vulgar, silent, too loud, aristocratic, or grotesque, they share in the radical detachment of representation that shows them as foreign, intruders, other. Perhaps Cortázar was, indeed, incapable of emulating Bioy Casares. The fable in Cortázar's writing is a shattering of the same mirror with which Bioy Casares's work tries to examine its own failures and mirages.

A Rivalry

Like Borges, Bioy Casares works in the established tradition of focusing fiction on the adventure of an individual hero in pursuit or, even more typically for Bioy Casares, in flight of something. If Borges's "The Intruder" affords us a model for the murderous implications of male friendship against all odds, "An Encounter in Rauch" in Bioy Casares's recent volume *A Russian Doll*[14] poses the issue of male rivalry with a different resolution.

The year is 1929. A young man goes on a business mission that requires him to spend a brief time at a hotel before resuming his trip; it is Christmas Eve and one of the guests sharing the table with him, a European, marvels at the fact that he has a business appointment on a day that should be observed as a holiday.

The young man, a somewhat insecure fellow who admits to having gotten and preserved his job thanks to his family's connections, balks at the idea that this guest, who remains unnamed throughout the story, may not believe in the seriousness of his assignment. As the evening proceeds, the young man is put off further by the condescension and politeness displayed by the more mature European, who engages him in a discussion about the function of faith in God and lying in an attempt to debunk the young man's rather curt dismissal of religion, ritual, and God. The description of the European as having a somewhat repellent otherworldly look, the kind that "is found in pictures of saints," reinforces the differences between the two and the inexplicably intense rivalry that becomes apparent in their discussion.

When, because of the rain, the European asks the young man for a ride—even though they are warned that the driving will be treacherous—the young man agrees reluctantly. Their ride through swamps is punctuated by the European forcing the young man to improve his driving so that he will not be outperformed by his foreign companion, who exhibits an irritating willingness to take control of the car as well as of the metaphysical aspect of their exchange. During this ride the young man has to contend with both the rain and a rival pushing him to drive better, argue more astutely, and watch the road more attentively. The story ends as the young man gets out of the car once the rain is over and fails to see anything but the flat countryside and the pampas surrounding him; there is no trace of his rival.

The rival has left after he succeeds in taking control of the trip and instilling disturbing doubts in the young man. In this Christmas story, the nonbeliever is taught a lesson about the unexplainable; he has been changed because he cannot triumph over an absent interlocutor. The power, again, lies with those further removed from experience. Like the silent Faustine, the rival has been able to elicit an adventure that would not have taken place without him. Absent, otherworldly, and irritating, the rival's foreignness typifies the productive unevenness of true misencounters. Love for a woman and male rivalry become the ultimate points in a representation that posits the conditions of its distancing as its own wisdom.

Notes

1. From Julio Cortázar, "Diario para un cuento," in *Deshoras* (México: Editorial Nueva Imagen, 1983), p. 135; my translation.
2. Jorge Luis Borges, in his preface to Adolfo Bioy Casares's *La invención de Morel* (Buenos Aires: Losada, 1940). I quote from Ruth L. Simms's translation in Adolfo Bioy Casares, *The Invention of Morel and Other Stories* (Austin: Univer-

sity of Texas Press, 1985), p. 6; page numbers of quoted passages follow this edition. Although on the whole this is an apt translation, there are places where I have changed it slightly to follow my sense of the original text. I prefer *Morel's Invention* for the title, and I refer to the novel by that title in this chapter. Suzanne Jill Levine explores the relationship between texts by Borges and by Bioy Casares in this early period in "Adolfo Bioy Casares y Jorge Luis Borges: La utopía como texto," *Revista Iberoamericana* 43 (July–December 1977): 415–32. See also her *Guía de Adolfo Bioy Casares* (Madrid: Fundamentos, 1982).

3. See "Tlön, Uqbar, Orbis Tertius," in Borges's *Ficciones*. Mention is made there of Bioy Casares's house and the role he plays in the scrutiny of the encyclopedia at issue in the story. Some of the works by Borges and Bioy Casares were published under pseudonyms: H. Bustos Domecq is the one chosen for *Seis problemas para don Isidoro Parodi* (1942) and *Dos fantasías memorables* (1946); Suárez Lynch is given as the author of *Un modelo para la muerte* (1946). Under their own names they jointly published *Los orilleros: El paraíso de los creyentes* (1955), *Crónicas de Bustos Domecq* (1967), and *Nuevos cuentos de Bustos Domecq* (1977) as well as an anthology of *gauchesco* (cowboy) literature. These works are collected in Jorge Luis Borges, *Obras completas en colaboración* (Buenos Aires: Emecé, 1979).

4. Juan Carlos Onetti is evoked because Cortázar is working in a neighborhood of Buenos Aires closely related to the atmosphere of prostitutes and sinister stories favored by Onetti. See Juan Carlos Onetti, *Obras completas* (Madrid: Aguilar, 1970), *La muerte y la niña* (Buenos Aires: Editorial Corregidor, 1973), *Tan triste como ella y otros cuentos* (Barcelona: Lumen, 1976), *Dejemos hablar al viento* (Barcelona: Bruguera, 1979), and *Cuentos secretos* (Montevideo: Marcha, 1986).

5. See Jacques Derrida, *La vérité en peinture* (Paris: Flammarion, 1978).

6. Daniel Martino in his *ABC de Adolfo Bioy Casares* (Alcalá de Henares: Ediciones de la Universidad, 1991) gives a detailed listing of the works of Bioy Casares that have been adapted for film. These films add an interesting dimension to the themes discussed in this book. Borges and Bioy Casares wrote screenplays with Hugo Santiago for *Invasión* (Buenos Aires, 1969) and *Les autres* (Paris: Bourgeois, 1974).

7. See E. T. A. Hoffmann, "The Sandman," trans. L. J. Kent and E. C. Knight, in Victor Lange, ed., *Tales* (New York: Continuum, 1982). Alain Robbe-Grillet is a longtime admirer of *Morel's Invention,* whose influence on his work is visible in both his cinematic and his written work. See Alain Robbe-Grillet, "Adolfo Bioy Casares: *L'invention de Morel,*" *Critique* 69 (February 1963). For a study of Bioy Casares's narrative strategies in his early period, consult Maribel Tamargo, *La narrativa de Bioy Casares: El texto como escritura-lectura* (Madrid: Playor, 1983).

8. Adolfo Bioy Casares, *Plan de evasión* (Buenos Aires: Galerna, 1969), trans. Suzanne Jill Levine, *Plan for Escape*. For further analysis of this work, see my "*Plan de evasión* de Adolfo Bioy Casares: La representación de la representación," in Donald Yates, ed., *Otros mundos, otros fuegos: Fantasía y realismo mágico en Iberoamérica* (East Lansing: Michigan State University, Latin American Studies Center, 1975).

9. This story is included in the English translation of *La invención de Morel*.

10. See Louis Auguste Blanqui, *Instructions pour une prise d'armes: L'éternité par les astres et autres textes* (Paris: Société Encyclopédique Française et Éditions de la Tête de Feuilles, 1972).

11. Adolfo Bioy Casares, *Dormir al sol* (Buenos Aires: Emecé, 1973), trans. Suzanne Jill Levine, *Asleep in the Sun* (New York: Persea Books, 1978). Page numbers are in accordance with the cited translation.

12. Adolfo Bioy Casares, *La aventura de un fotógrafo en La Plata* (Buenos Aires: Emecé, 1985); my translation; page numbers are in accordance with the cited Spanish edition. See José Miguel Oviedo, "*La aventura de un fotógrafo en La Plata,*" *Vuelta* 120 (November 1986): 58–60.

13. Adolfo Bioy Casares, *El héroe de las mujeres* (Madrid: Alfaguara, 1979); my translation; page numbers are in accordance with the cited Spanish edition. For another perspective on the female representations in the work of Bioy Casares, see José Miguel Oviedo, "Angeles abominables: Las mujeres en las historias fantásticas de Bioy Casares," in his *Escrito al margen* (Bogotá: Procultura, 1982). Enrique Pezzoni notes the role played by irony in Bioy Casares's representation of love in earlier works. See Enrique Pezzoni, "Bioy Casares: Adversos milagros," in his *El escritor y sus voces* (Buenos Aires: Sudamericana, 1986), pp. 237–45.

14. Adolfo Bioy Casares, "Encuentro en Rauch," in his *Una muñeca rusa* (Barcelona: Tusquets, 1991).

Chapter 6
Is There Style Without Gender? Manuel Puig

> The man-mad man is not mad about men per se, as one might think from his name, he is really keen on the qualities of men. He seeks these qualities, he appropriates them, he belongs to them. There is no boldness, there is no strength that he does not espy, track down and swallow. Those who are defeated go unnoticed, for him the world is made up of winners.
> —Elias Canetti, *Ear Witness*[1]

> I am not so happy to day in the recollection of last evening's entertainment, as I was in the enjoyment.
> —Hannah W. Foster, *The Coquette*[2]

The Politics of Winning

The man-mad man *belongs* to the qualities that make men win. He only associates with winners. The contempt that Elias Canetti feels for the character he has drawn is clear; this caricature of the self-confident man who knows "every mercenary personally" and who "grabbed his plane and arrived on time . . . risked danger, concluded treaties and flew off to the next war" is an implicit acceptance of the opposite of this amoral winner. The efficiency and clarity of the goals he pursues lead this man-mad man to arrive at the inevitable conclusion: "everyone knows that there are too many people, and men are supposed to get rid of the superfluous ones" (p. 95).

Manuel Puig drew patiently the profile of the man-mad man's opposite, one who does not want to win in mercenary terms, the one who not only does not understand the terms of the wars being fought but even manages to arrive at the wrong time. *The Kiss of the Spider Woman*[3] is many tales but, above all, it is a story of mismatchings. The basic situation of the novel is well known, thanks to the film of the same title. Two characters, Molina and Arregui, sit in an Argentine jail during the years of extreme persecution of the left and all those loosely defined as subversive. Molina's reasons for incarceration are not explicitly political; he is homosexual and has been accused of corrupting minors. Arregui, an activist of Marxist persuasion and a heterosexual, is imprisoned for his clandestine political activities.

Molina is a film enthusiast. For him, movies are a source of pleasure, personal projection, and sexual arousal. Political discourse bores him and seems ultimately unimportant to him. His life is animated by details, small gestures, and sentimental scenes.[4] The two men pass their time talking about films that Molina tells in great detail to Arregui; eventually the films become a polemical matrix for them. Molina and Arregui are able to spell out their personal differences around the reactions they have to particular films. Molina begins this interchange:

—"What an enigmatic ending, isn't it?"
—"No, it's fine, it's the best part of the movie."
—"And why?"
—"Because it means that although she is left with nothing, she is happy that she was able to have one true relationship in her life, even though it's over."
—"But doesn't one suffer more, after having been happy and being left with nothing?"
—"Molina, there's one thing to keep in mind. In a man's life, whether it's short or long, everything is provisional. Nothing is forever."
—"Yes, but at least let it last a little bit."
—"One should be able to accept things as they come, and appreciate the good things that happen to you even if they don't last. Because nothing is forever."
—"Yes, that's easy to say. But feeling it is something else." (p. 263)

The recounting of films reveals the dual nature of the information communicated in any conversation; the interlocutors become involved in their developing bond even as they appear to be discussing neutral events in the past. Molina and Arregui are caught in the logic of an exchange that draws them closer and leads to their having sexual relations.

Molina's triumph is his seduction of Arregui. He is able to make him see the limitations of his explanations concerning human behavior and his own sexuality. In Arregui's vision, class struggle and love between men and women prevail. He has a clear moral and political conscience and seems to be sure of the role that he plays, as an individual, in the larger world perspective. Arregui's world is dialectical, teleological, eminently explainable, and open to change by revolutionary action. Even though he is in jail, being tortured, and asked to give out information about his clandestine activities, he thinks that he knows the reasons behind the violence. He is a victim but does not conceive of himself as being blindly moved by chance.

Molina is a sentimental, middle class, male homosexual with ideals close to those pictures of family life found in fifties films. He wants a stable relationship with a stronger man whom he can comfort and admire; his role in that couple would be that of the flattering, supportive wife. Molina years for stability and happiness. His view of life is essentially nostalgic and ahistorical. If he is uncomfortable with the status quo, it is only because, being a male, the kind of role he would like to have can be pursued only at personal risk.

Molina is not a transgressive homosexual like Jean Genet; these jail scenes have little to do with *Notre Dame des Fleurs*.[5] Their aim is to emphasize the beauty of an unattainable goal: the middle class household.

Neither Molina nor Arregui is completely aware of what is happening to them. Arregui does not know that his cellmate has been placed there by the police in order to extract information about his activities and companions, and Molina cannot be sure that the deal that he struck with the police—allowing him to walk out with a lighter sentence in exchange for his work—will be honored. The police give poisoned food to Arregui so that he will be physically weakened and become more vulnerable to Molina's friendship and curiosity. The food provokes vomiting and diarrhea, and provides an occasion for Molina to take care of him and show him friendship. In a gesture that suggests the sentimental investment Molina has in the situation, he gives food that is brought for him from the outside to Arregui so that he may be spared at least some discomfort.

The reader learns about the role of the police through a dialogue, presented in an official report, between Molina and the Director of the prison:

> Director: Was it helpful to weaken him physically?
> Defendant: The first dish that was brought in I had to eat myself.
> Director: Why? You shouldn't have done that. . . .
> Defendant: Well, because he doesn't like polenta. And since one plate had more than the other . . . he insisted I have the biggest one, and it would have sounded suspicious if I had refused. You told me that the one that was specially prepared would come in the newer tin plate, but they made the mistake of putting too much in it. And I had to eat it myself.
> Director: Ah, very well, Molina. I congratulate you. I apologize for our mistake.
> Defendant: Maybe that's why you see me thinner, I've been sick for two days.
> Director: And Arregui? How is his morale? Have we been able to soften him up a bit? What do you think?
> Defendant: Yes, but perhaps it would be best to let him pull himself back together a bit. (p. 153)

Thus Molina gains his status as the star of the novel, with all the Hollywood connotations of the word when translated into the vocabulary of larger-than-life heroines, such as those played by Joan Crawford, Marlene Dietrich, and Bette Davis. He is also capable of depth and contradiction: he may be either covering up for Arregui or capable of fatally betraying him. His dedication to caring for Arregui may be the result of true abnegation or strategic manipulation. All eyes are on Molina. Will he, out of love, save Arregui from the hooks of his torturers? Or will he give him up so that he may resume his life in the outside world?

When Molina and Arregui have intercourse in the cell, Arregui tries to convince Molina that being a homosexual does not necessarily imply that Molina should let himself be overwhelmed by another male, a "macho." Molina says that he is happy with his sexuality, which he defines as being that of a "middle class woman." He wants the man to rule. Their relationship has been constituted as a romance; Arregui allows Molina to kiss him, an important gesture that elevates their sexual encounter to a higher plane.

As Molina's date for leaving prison approaches, the two men decide that Molina will take a message to Arregui's associates outside. It is the culmination of their romance. They kiss while making love; this will be their last encounter.

The two last chapters of the novel consist of a police report about Molina's activities, attesting to the fact that he had been followed from the moment he left and was killed before being able to give the information sent by Arregui, together with a scene of Arregui who, badly tortured, lapses into a delirium that takes him into a recollection of movies and past conversations with Molina. The enigma about the motivation behind Molina's actions still haunts the reader through the police report:

". . . he may have been trying to escape with the extremists or he may have been ready to be eliminated by them." (p. 279)

Who has won? Molina is portrayed with the prestige of the victim. Misunderstood by society and by those who want to change it, he is nevertheless capable of dying for love. Molina has fought a battle against Canetti's man-mad men and, in his failure to be like them, he achieves what the novel offers as the triumph of his stardom.

Culture and Consumption

Borges's *Aleph* has taught us the extent to which sequential language betrays what it wants to convey. Although our reading of *The Kiss of the*

Spider Woman is faithful to what may be perceived when we pay attention only to plot, we have lost the *rest,* in its dual meaning of what is left: a residue, and what is superfluous.

The Kiss of the Spider Woman is a novel that consists almost completely of materials that are apparently residues from other sources. The story itself, with a homosexual man who dies for love in an act of heroism, has the sentimentality of Hollywood productions coupled with a hyperrealism that calls its verisimilitude into question. The linear retelling of the plot has affinities with Arregui's attitude toward Molina's retelling of the films: he would have liked him to move swiftly from beginning to end, overlooking details and bringing the films to their sociological and political implications. In brief, as we consume the novel in this way, we try to use it for something else while we remain blinded to the implications of its architecture.

Molina's retelling of the films presents one of the alternatives for reading; he stops at details, forgets the path that may lead him to the ending, and succeeds in having Arregui weave his own life into the spaces opened up by his renditions. Thus narrating is conceived as a weaving that criss-crosses separate temporal experiences: having seen the films, having lived, and the present tense seduction of the dialogue.

When Molina and Arregui start speaking about their own lives during their discussions about movies, they take the road of interpretation. As they project themselves in the movies, they build alternative plots, fill in the blanks in the psychology of the characters, and, in short, understand the films in terms of an interpretative code that seems to be related to their own experiences.

The films are also tools for dismantling lies. Arregui is shown to have misrepresented the extent of his attraction to the active, independent woman who is his companion, since he is drawn in films to those middle class heroines in whom Molina projects himself. The films are a persuasive network that envelops Arregui and makes him fall for Molina at the same time that he is able to discover something about himself. It is, then, impossible to consume the movies, that is, to appropriate them and remain unchanged. Their retelling only emphasizes their absence by showing us that the *present* tense of the conversation is a parasite of other discourses, inscribed in its margins.

The actual subjects discussed by the characters become mere pretexts for that other, unspoken plot being developed without words but through evocations of something else. Molina and Arregui cannot properly be said to consume the films; they are, instead, being consumed by the movies' discursive machinery.

The cell makes disinterested dialogue impossible. Each of the interlocutors has one or several ulterior motives: Molina his own arrangement with the police; Arregui his desire to have Molina fulfill a revolutionary mission; the police their ever-watchful vigilance. Everything said is framed and redefined by the system imposed by incarceration. The cell grants meaning to the words.

Bioy Casares speaks in *A Plan for Escape* about a cell enclosed by mirrors that produce a "hot horror," part of a contrived plot of conspiracies carefully enclosed in the limited cell made to lose its true dimensions by the mirrors.[6] In relation to such a blindness about the place and its borders, an impossibility of retaining proprietary relations with one's utterances, *The Kiss of the Spider Woman* offers us its own mirroring as temporal. It is the temporality of the inmates' discourse that makes them face up to the fact that regardless of what they are trying to convey with their words, they can only articulate through them time and again their own condition as prisoners, their present tense.

What are the men telling, then? Molina and Arregui, in fascist Buenos Aires, articulate a discourse that they think they control but that is being watched and generated by the police. They exchange cultural fragments that reproduce the conditions of their imprisonment. There is no need for Molina to "politicize" his accounts, as Arregui would like. He may get lost in details, dream himself a panther-woman, star in Nazi films. The novel weaves the elements together through the hypothesis of a consumer, the police, and produces its own reading. Thus no element in the dialogue between the two men may be construed as central; they all share in their residual or parasitic status.

Recounting the novel becomes one of the instances of consumption being denied to its characters. The strong reading takes us from the wish of encapsulating a plot to the curiosity about whether we may understand how our own exercise is being told from the privileged position we hold as readers. The unavoidable result leads us to the police and their ever-watchful manipulative eye.

The Pedagogical Moment

The Kiss of the Spider Woman is interspersed with footnotes explaining homosexual behavior from the point of view of several thinkers, above all the ego psychologist Otto Fenichel. The notes repeat in a flat and informative tone clinical notions about homosexuality; they appear in counterpoint with the conversations between Molina and Arregui so that if we read them, they may be considered an explanation. But *The Kiss of the Spider Woman* has a different design for them. Caught as we are by the relationship between the two men, the notes appear to be an instance of disciplinary discourse that conspires against the intensity of the men's bond. Overdetermined by the sentimentality of the effects of the romance, the reader is effectively urged to abandon the openly pedagogical discourse and submit to the novel in a way akin to Molina's film viewing.

Police and pedagogical discourses are equated and dismissed; the alternative is the difficult disassembling talent of Molina that allows him to find the unacceptable—tenderness in the Nazi film heroine—by stripping her of plot and history and willingness to strike deals with the police, so that he can have a love affair. Rather than love conquering all, Molina's is a love conquered by all.[7]

Sentimentality, an interest in plot, gossip, and deceit permeate the almost suffocating intimacy of Puig's novels as he tries to situate their language close to the pleasures elicited by the sources of popular culture they evoke. In *Heartbreak Tango*[8] several women are engaged in an exchange of letters. Their bond is stated simply: a newspaper from a provincial town announces the untimely death of a young man, Juan Carlos Etchepare. His mother and an old girlfriend, Nené (now married and living in the "city" with her husband and children), write to each other impelled by the nostalgia elicited by Juan Carlos's death. It is later revealed that Juan Carlos's sister, Celina, had been the actual author of the letters received by Nené, which she had signed with her mother's name. The subject of the novel shifts from an interest in the explicit retrospective materials, presented by the letters, to the reasons for the hoax. A hatred between women suggested through the conceit is presented as more pressing than the love between Nené and Juan Carlos.

The dream of utmost happiness in *Heartbreak Tango* is serene domesticity but, when achieved by Nené through marriage to a dependable husband, it appears flat and gray. In contrast, her infatuation with Juan Carlos is a measure of her capacity to have lived a higher form of love, almost an aesthetic denial of her present family. Tango lyrics, used as epigraphs in each chapter, tinge the women's conflict with irony and a sense of inevitability.

Juan Carlos, the dead man, succumbed to the ravages of an illness that—in the best tradition of literary attractiveness—caused him to get thinner and cough up blood. He is an enigmatic point of convergence for the sense of unease that Nené feels about her conventional married life and the driving resentment of the unmarried Celina, who has become a schoolteacher. Juan Carlos embodies beauty and eroticism, whereas the women have been left with mere fragments, recollections of a past youth in a world cluttered by unfulfilled expectations (the schoolteacher Celina) and the boredom of being a housewife (Nené).

The hatred that Celina feels for Nené matches the hostility that

Nené feels for her. As the reader realizes the hoax on which the exchange of letters is based, the novel betrays its "real" subject: the suspicion that love will always be outside women's discourse. Juan Carlos's death is only a pretext for uncovering their own lack of daring. Even a provincial Casanova—Juan Carlos was a handsome heartbreaker of little intelligence—has enough power to show the inadequacy of women in relation to their object of desire.

Is this all a joke? Are the letters, the sentimentality, the tangos described so that we may laugh? And, in that case, what would be the nature of our laughter? Puig's work as a whole is open to this sort of inquiry. *Heartbreak Tango* is persistent in its opacity regarding these issues; when summarized it yields humorous results and when read it resists any distancing from its sentimentality. If there is a joke here, then, it is on the reader, who is caught in the same web as the characters.

The laughter is self-critical, an awareness of having been seduced. *Heartbreak Tango* leads us to its overall effect of women lying to each other (through the death of a man handsome but ridiculous) in a language articulated by a relentless common sense. As tangos often relate, part of the sadness is that the love object, while not meriting the passion she elicits, is still infinitely more desirable than the person who pursues her. Puig fashions a reversal of the tango tradition, because here the love object is a man rather than a woman.

In *Heartbreak Tango* letters become what they perhaps always are: objects through which the characters attempt to create a presence for themselves in the hope of overwhelming the recipient, of according credence to something that might become true if the recipient accepted the invitation to continue the game and respond to the letters. This kind of a game is a signing exercise, in which each letter is a dare to continue the exchange. The identities generated owe their solidarity to their faithfulness to the letter, to the coherence with which they cling to the univocality of their signatures. Letters are characters and they make up characters; it is the seduction of the characters represented and produced by the signatures that keeps the story going. The *fact* of the letter exchange is an *effect* that gives presence to the signature.

The epigraph to the opening chapter of *Heartbreak Tango* in its English edition is a fragment from Homero Manzi's tango "Su voz" (His Voice):

> The shadows on the dance floor
> this tango brings sad memories to mind
> let us dance and think no more
> while my satin dress
> like a tear shines.

As in the tango, the novel is centered on the active forgetting of a supposedly unforgettable memory. In these lyrics by Manzi, one of the most nostalgic poets of tango, the dancers are shadows propelled by a memory they want to erase even as they affirm it, because the very genre of their dance constitutes a remembrance of their loss. The novel unfolds the image of a satin dress like a tear in a retrospective and sentimental key.

The satin dress is indeed like a tear: one wears one's sorrow. The attire makes emotion visible and embodies it; it creates the right character for the dance. The correspondence among feeling, identity, and movement alluded to in these lines is an ideal searched for throughout Puig's novel. But such an easy, natural relationship to their medium of expression is denied to the female characters, who are trapped by the insufficiency of the commonplaces they are seemingly destined to use.

Once the novel has established a place for Juan Carlos's body ("The remains of Juan Carlos Etchepare were interred in the local burial ground, accompanied to their final home by a grief-stricken funeral cortege"), the first letter is sent by Juan Carlos's old love, Nené. Its stated purpose is to send condolences to Mrs. Etchepare, Juan Carlos's mother. Through the letter we learn that Nené lives now in Buenos Aires, has a husband and two children, and had not seen Juan Carlos for nine years. We also learn about a vague, unresolved problem between Nené and Celina and Mrs. Etchepare:

I've been living in Buenos Aires for several years now, soon after I got married I came to live here with my husband, but this terrible news made me decide to drop you a few lines in spite of the fact that before my marriage yourself and your daughter Celina had stopped speaking to me. In spite of everything poor Juan Carlos always said hello to me, may he rest in peace. (p. 10)

The letters that follow build an entanglement among three characters. Celina, trying to get even with Nené after years of resentment, poses as her own mother by forging her signature. For Nené, what is explicitly at issue in the letters is the consecration of her past with Juan Carlos. She believes that the correspondence is the equivalent of erecting a monument for him: a loving girlfriend on one side and an aching mother on the other construct a friendship from the remains of their love and passion for a now dead man. Much is said in the novel about Juan Carlos's body. He is so attractive that he is irresistible; he is a womanizer of such kindness that he leaves behind only love for him in the women he conquers.

Old letters written by Juan Carlos are presented as an archaeology of the female correspondence that frames them; they suggest the quality of Juan Carlos's presence in the past evoked by the letter-writing after his death. They perform this function in a curious way, having to do with his identity as an author, with his signature. Although Nené and Celina (the main correspondents) write well, with no spelling mistakes and the correctness of good students, Juan Carlos's writing abounds in spelling errors and capricious punctuation. He writes like an ignorant and unimaginative school dropout.[9]

What is the effect of such "bad writing" on the perception of Juan Carlos as a character? The most immediate one is the production of a strong novelistic presence for him. He does not need to write about anything in a correct way; his task is fulfilled by merely *presenting* himself; he sounds more pure, less literary than the characters who mention him.

The errors in writing, with the compassionate laughter that they elicit in the reader, the colloquial turns of phrase taken from the realm of the commonplace, are evidence of Juan Carlos's uncomfortable relationship to literature—the only medium through which we know him. The reader suspects that there is more to him, that the chunks of public language he is obliged to recycle in his letters are but a pale indication of his persona. By exaggerating Juan Carlos's inadequacy with language, Puig emphasizes another level that remains all the more intense because of its invisibility: Juan Carlos's body.

Juan Carlos does not need to write well. He is the first character in the novel to have achieved centrality in an event: his own death. Death constitutes the achievement of the illusion of presence and tangibility in the politics of interaction of *Heartbreak Tango*. The dead body is the decisive point of interlocution, very much like the absent films in *Kiss of the Spider Woman*. His letters stand as a confirmation of the fact that Juan Carlos will not write any more, but they are also, most of all, confirmation of him as a *fact*.

Unlike that of Juan Carlos Celina's and Nené's identities waver. Celina forges her mother's signature and initiates the most explicit lie in the novel; she signs as another. In contrast, by signing with her own name, Nené discovers that she would rather *be* another.

The novel closes with another body; Nené's signature is unfolded and delivered of the vagueness it carried throughout the novel when she dies. In this way she becomes, like Juan Carlos, central in an event. Juan Carlos's old letters are burnt in agreement with her will (old letters that she wanted to take with her to her grave right until the day she died, when she seemingly attained a more singular self-definition). This change of mind means that her death is not the death of the Nené who signed the letters we read but of someone quite different. Juan Carlos's letters are again transcribed in the novel, this time in fragments, as they fly up into the air before turning into ashes, thereby creating a highly sentimental retrospective account of what we have read.

Only one among the characters of the epistolary exchange remains alive at the novel's end. It is Celina, the schoolteacher with enough mastery of the language to forge letters, incapable of becoming a character with the kind of weight that, we are told in *Heartbreak Tango,* only death can achieve. Hers is the power of plotting, of initiating a correspondence of which she will always be in control. Thus the winner of the interlocutionary exercise of this novel is a participant whose victory is achieved by a most intense understanding of the nature of letter-writing, so precise that she can manipulate the conventions of the genre by forgery.

Manuel Puig has offered us in these two novels the figures of two supreme and hateful puppeteers: the police in *The Kiss of the Spider Woman* and the schoolteacher in *Heartbreak Tango.* It matters little that the characters think they understand their own designs and those of others: institutionalized knowledge looks over their shoulders and, with a somber wink to the reader, rearranges the meaning of their words and inflects their voices without their knowledge.

Fragments

Pieces of paper tossed up in the air in *Heartbreak Tango,* chunks of conversations and movies passing swiftly in Arregui's delirium: these are only the most explicitly fragmented materials to enter Manuel Puig's work. His novels are constituted as a collection of fragments. The abundance of dialogue, seldom interrupted by a narrator (*The Kiss of the Spider Woman, Heartbreak Tango, Betrayed by Rita Hayworth,*[10] *Eternal Curse on the Reader of These Pages,*[11] *Blood of Requited Love,*[12] and *Tropical Night Falling*[13] are cases in point), supplemented by such other materials as police reports, school compositions, and letters, make his novels a kind of collage held together by common sense. No matter how disparate the elements he may choose to combine or how surprising their joint inclusion might seem, the privileged reading is sentimental and prudently down to earth, even in its wildest dreams.

Pubis Angelical[14] is Manuel Puig's most ambitious attempt at combining different layers of representation in a single work. Dialogue located in the contemporary reality of Latin America, film sequences from decades past, and a fantasy of the future come together in one volume, all haunted by the same representation: women on the verge of death struggling reluctantly against a kind of power that oppresses them.

In one of the sequences belonging to the past, an actress who has been drugged by her older husband so that they could have intercourse is startled by a change in her attendant, Thea:

> The Mistress looked at her, startled. Thea took a few steps backward toward the opening of the tent. It was impossible to scrutinize the expression on her face because she was against the light, behind her the glare crept between the flaps of the opening. And then it was the Mistress who drew back, in horror, when she saw that Thea had also begun to disrobe, while saying in a voice which grew deeper and deeper, "I prepared that cup in a moment of misconduct, of foolish lust." Thea's silhouette was revealing itself to be more and more lean, the legs were profiled as muscular and covered with down, "But I will not copy your husband's cowardice, I will not avail myself of that narcotic. I want to place myself in front of you, such as I am, and allow you to decide." When the last item of clothing had been removed, with a whack she wrenched off the wig, a mane pulled back tautly in a low chignon, lifted one of the many rags off the ground and began to wipe the makeup off her face. One of these motions placed her in profile, and the Mistress, with enormous respect and unexpected relief, observed that Thea was a man. (p. 53)

The Mistress witnesses the change in Thea "with enormous respect." The relief and respect have to do with the sense of modesty that moves Puig's characters in *Pubis Angelical* as well as in his other works. Lesbian sex would have been too much of a transgression; heterosexual sex in the form of adultery against a conniving and unattractive husband—presented in the novel as a caricature of von Stroheim with a reference to the enigmatic power he holds over weaker, younger females such as we have seen in *Foolish Wives*—is seen as due revenge.

Thea's gender is an extreme disguise: dowdy and severe female attendant during her usual chores and sexy male lover in the "reality" underneath the clothes and makeup. Thea and the Mistress experience Thea's transvestism as a thrill and the danger they both run as a form of heroism. But why the respect?

The Mistress is drawn to manly qualities; she performs in *Pubis Angelical* the role of the typical actress of von Stroheim's time: beautiful, fragile, and attracted by men who can overwhelm her even as they prove to be good, better than a rapist. Always in danger of being violated or killed by some monstrous or merely mean male figure, these female characters give themselves up willingly to lovers who are also protectors, deliverers from the dangers they face.

The scene of a vulnerable female, whose goodness is inferred from the fact of her vulnerability, traverses Puig's novels as a founding fantasy and a lost paradise. The sentimental value of films being told in his novels often derives from seeing these females defeated but preserving their dignity. Puig quotes and invents these situations repeatedly, with the sort of respect with which the Mistress watches Thea become a man. The original love scene resides in this unevenness in the couple, in having one look at the other from an elevated place, just as the character in *Morel's Invention* does with a wink to the reader. There is no wink about this situation in Manuel Puig's work. If the effect is often excessively maudlin and appears to be funny, the laughter does not erase the importance it has as a key to Puig's theater of emotion.

When Molina is killed in *The Kiss of the Spider Woman,* he attains the martyrdom of femaleness. Like Thea, he is able to change as the situation shifts, stripping him of his male homosexuality to turn him into a female star of the kind in films now considered nostalgia pieces.

Fragments of culture as they emerge in Puig's writing are the only elements given the characters to construct their identities. They are capable of losing and exchanging these fragments precisely because they are distinct pieces. In the rearrangement of the pieces there is no aristocratic effort, they belong to everybody. Their origin is extremely humble: movies, magazines, tangos, boleros, everyday Argentine speech.

Manuel Puig had possessed a respect for the movies of the past in their most melodramatic effects. He was able to assume the personality of an actress for hours on end and talk using her voice and personality as though the films in which she was cast had effectively produced a persona temporarily inhabiting his own. He was particularly taken with Lana Turner, whose character in *Madame X* moved him to tears each time he saw the film. Guillermo Cabrera Infante, in a remarkable obituary published after Manuel Puig's untimely death, recalls an episode involving Lana Turner:

Manuel did not have ideology but he had idolatries. His faithful old friend, Néstor Almendros, stumbled onto one. He arrived in New York late one night and called Manuel, who did not sleep. "Come here and stay in my apartment." Néstor, already in his hotel, was reluctant. "Come and talk to me about film and fashion." Néstor agreed. Already in the apartment, which was the size of a closet, he brought in his luggage and talked with Manuel. Suddenly they came to Lana Turner. Manuel said he adored her, which was true, Néstor said he detested her, which was also true. All of a sudden, Manuel opened the door and said to Néstor: "A person who hates Lana cannot stay under my roof"—and at three in the morning he threw him out into the unfriendly New York streets.[15]

Tinkering with pieces of culture was not only a way for constructing novels, but foremost for Manuel Puig, it was the building of an eminently nostalgic self. The makeup and the characters played by the actors were more important than the actual lives they might be leading. This project was also one he applied to his own person. As an intellectual, Manuel Puig viewed and represented the world as it already came represented by the nonliterary media. He was the exact opposite of Borges in his choice of elements, but maintained a faithfulness to his references that reminds us of Borges's own relationship to libraries and deceased writers.

When Thea takes off her clothes and is revealed as a man, we enter a figuration of gender mirages that has its most intense representation in a passage from *Pubis Angelical*:

And she got to her feet and asked, raising her voice as much as she could, where was her daughter. But no one knew what to answer her, the shooting grew more severe and the soldiers were being ordered to load up with more and more gunpowder. Suddenly a strange gust of wind arose and the nightdress was lifted, showing me to be naked, and the men trembled, and it's that they saw that I was a divine creature, my pubis was like that of angels, without down and without sex. (p. 231)

Nakedness is again greeted with respect, this time even with awe. In the midst of an apocalyptic scenario, a skirt is lifted, recalling the well-known Marilyn Monroe pose, and the sex that is not one appears for all to behold. The fighting stops; the version has a healing quality. The angelical pubis is not a recollection but a working and fleeting hypothesis, a necessary point in Puig's sustained reflection about gender.

Gender identity is defined in Puig's work by the clothes, makeup, and roles one is allowed to play by recurrent fragments of culture. The quotation from *Pubis Angelical* stands as a parareligious figuration that vanishes in the novel to give way to a universe still offering only two genders.

If the attributes of gender, the feminine or virile looks, are examined in Puig's writing, there is also the conviction that the look is what we must take as the essence; the configuration of the fragments may be temporary but it is also weighty and stands for whatever depth is to be found. In this vision there is a grounding force, a language that overrides the difficulties and artificiality of others, its middle class Argentine, feminine inflected chatter. The leading fantasy for Molina and so many other characters in Puig's work is to be a middle class woman. Although the goal is unattainable as such, the novels are told with female middle class inflections in the leading role.

It is through such mainstream voices that the reader recognizes that the battle for truth has been won. Puig's novels—not perceived as representing styles of speech but as the actual expression of reality—attain what his characters cannot: to be an embodiment of what is at stake for the author in mainstream Latin American women. *Cae la noche tropical* is offered as a composite picture of female dialogues; the son who wants to take care of his aging mother by making her move to Europe with him and away from Brazil, where she has female friends, is read as an intruder.

The reader, interested in the gossip, the intimacy of the conversations, and the results of spying, does not want the women to stop talking. Through their chatter, the lessons of everyday sentimental defeats and triumphs are told. Removed from the big issues, their style, reassuring and prudent, weaves what Manuel Puig's work gives us as truth.

Notes

1. Elias Canetti, *Ear Witness: Fifty Characters*, trans. Joachim Neugroschel (New York: Farrar, Straus, Giroux, 1986), p. 94. The original title is *Der Ohrenzeuge: Funfzig Charaktere*.

2. Hannah W. Foster, *The Coquette* (New York: Oxford University Press, 1986), p. 19. The first American edition of this book dates from 1797.

3. Manuel Puig, *El beso de la mujer araña* (Barcelona: Seix Barral, 1979). Page numbers cited are in accordance with this edition; the translation is mine.

4. For studies on the films told by Molina, see Pamela Bacarisse, *The Necessary Dream* (Totowa, NJ: Barnes and Noble, 1988), Francine Masiello, "Jailhouse Flicks: Projections by Manuel Puig," *Symposium* 32 (Spring 1978): 15–25, and Lucille Kerr, *Suspended Fictions: Reading Novels by Manuel Puig* (Urbana: University of Illinois Press, 1987).

5. Molina is not attracted to the marginality of homosexuals in society. On the contrary, he would like to be accepted into a mainstream that may only exist, because of its conservatism, in his dreams. Stephanie Merrim's "For a New (Psychological) Novel in the Works of Manuel Puig," *Novel* 17 (Winter 1984): 141–57, offers a perceptive analysis of the narrative intricacies present in Puig's psychological motifs. See also James R. Green, "*El beso de la mujer araña*: Sexual Repression and Textual Repression," *La Chispa 81: Selected Proceedings of the Louisiana Conference on Hispanic Languages and Literatures* (New Orleans: Tulane University, 1981), pp. 133–39.

6. See the edition of *Plan de evasión* cited in Chapter 5, devoted to Bioy Casares. Molina's film summaries perform a function akin to that of the mirrors in the Bioy Casares novel.

7. Molina is not humiliated by this radical defeat. Not being able "to make it" confirms his sense of an oblique kind of superiority over those not sensitive enough to understand the intricacies of love.

8. Manuel Puig, *Heartbreak Tango* (New York: E. P. Dutton, 1975), trans. Suzanne Jill Levine; page numbers are in accordance with this edition. The novel presents a consistent melodramatic register that approaches kitsch without causing the humorous reaction in the reader connected with such bad taste. See Julio Rodríguez Luis, "*Boquitas pintadas*: Folletín unanimista?" *Sin nombre* 5, 1 (1974): 50–56. Also Gustavo Pellón, "Manuel Puig's Contradictory Strategy: Kitsch Paradigms Versus Paradigmatic Strategies in *El beso de la mujer araña* and *Pubis Angelical*," *Symposium* 36 (1983): 186–201.

9. José Emilio Pacheco's short novel *El principio del placer* offers a feminine

character similar to Juan Carlos. Her bad spelling makes her all the more attractive to a young male protagonist who, like Nené and Celina, is a good student. It is as though ignorance of written language implies ready access to another, more physical and basic realm. José Emilio Pacheco, *El principio del placer* (México: Joaquín Mortiz, 1972). The women who compose the gallery of Angeles Mastretta's *Mujeres de ojos grandes* seem to be beyond any intellectual concern, which makes them, according to the logic of the stories in the volume, more focused on the trappings of love. Angeles Mastretta, *Mujeres de ojos grandes* (Buenos Aires: Planeta Sur, 1992).

10. Manuel Puig, *Betrayed by Rita Hayworth* (New York: Dutton, 1971); *La traición de Rita Hayworth* (Buenos Aires: Editorial Jorge Alvarez, 1968).

11. Manuel Puig, *Eternal Curse on the Reader of These Pages* (New York: Knopf, 1979); *Maldición eterna a quien lea estas páginas* (Barcelona: Seix Barral, 1980).

12. Manuel Puig, *Blood of Requited Love* (New York: Vintage, 1984); *Sangre de amor correspondido* (Barcelona: Seix Barral, 1982).

13. Manuel Puig, *Cae la noche tropical* (Barcelona: Seix Barral, 1988); *Tropical Night Falling* (New York, Norton, 1993);

14. Manuel Puig, *Pubis Angelical* (New York: Vintage 1986); *Pubis Angelical* (Barcelona: Seix Barral, 1979), trans. Elena Brunet, *Pubis Angelical: A Novel* (New York: Random House, 1986); page references are in accordance with the English edition.

15. Guillermo Cabrera Infante, "Manuel Puig," *El País* (July 24, 1990); my translation.

Chapter 7
The Lucidity of Inaction: María Luisa Bombal

> If Nathanael had had eyes for anything but the lovely Olympia, there would inevitably have been a number of disagreeable quarrels; for it was obvious that the carefully smothered laughter which broke out among the young people in this corner and that, was directed toward the lovely Olympia, whom they were watching curiously for an unknown reason. Heated by the quantity of wine he had drunk and by the dancing, Nathanael had cast off his characteristic shyness. He sat beside Olympia, her hand in his, and with fervor and passion he spoke of his love in words that no one could understand, neither he nor Olympia. But perhaps she did, for she sat with her eyes fixed upon his, sighing again and again, "Ah," "ah," "ah." Whereupon Nathanael answered: "Oh, you magnificent and heavenly woman! You ray shining from the promised land of love! You deep soul, in which my whole being is reflected" and more of the same. But Olympia did nothing but continue to sigh, "Ah, ah."
> —E. T. A. Hoffmann, "The Sandman"[1]

In *One Hundred Years of Solitude* García Márquez offered us in the character of Remedios the hypothesis of a fatal kind of female beauty endowed with an ability to speak literally, without recourse to metaphor. Remedios was considered to be of superior intelligence by some characters because of her capacity to engage directly, to utter unadorned, fundamental concepts grounded in the material world; to others she was merely retarded and unschooled.

Remedios's intuition and La Maga's gift for inscribing herself in the literature she reads while preserving her own identity are descriptions of the female condition possessing depth that relates to a privileged perception. Nathanael's mistake about Olympia's nature in Hoffmann's "The Sandman" is but one figuration of a long tradition viewing the lack of something in women as being compensated for by the emergence of something other, totally different, and eminently better.

Olympia is a doll. The characters who laugh at Nathanael when he approaches her and opens up his heart in passionate declarations may be right in their dismissal of Nathanael's blindness, but they have no access to the kind of self-absorption that allows him to take the lifeless Olympia for a real woman.

Olympia's silence, interrupted by sighs, has a seductive acquiescence that promises everything without uttering a word; her gaze opens up the vast possibilities dreamt by the protagonist of *Morel's Invention* regarding Faustine. In his blindness, Nathanael has entered a realm that will interpret him and eventually destroy him. The ultimate triumph of common sense in "The Sandman" does not solve the riddle about the kind of attraction elicited by Olympia. On the contrary, the ending of the story reads like a disappointing abandonment of what was most puzzling about its characters. The even tempered and commonsensical Klara is pictured in the following manner:

> Many years later it was reported that Klara had been seen in a remote district sitting hand in hand with a pleasnt-looking man in front of the door of a splendid country house, two merry boys playing around her. Thus it may be concluded that Klara eventually found that quiet, domestic happiness that her cheerful nature required and that Nathanael, with his lacerated soul, could never have provided her. (p. 308)

Klara's success evokes for the contemporary mind the kind of existence lived by Nené in *Heartbreak Tango*. Something is missing once the danger has been removed.

Olympia's embodiment of the feminine for Nathanael fulfills his desire to see himself in someone else. Her ever-watchful stare makes him long for more and more news about his own person. Olympia is uncritical, beautiful, and adoring, but the darkness of her secret, her lifelessness, threatens Nathanael's very existence. The evocation of feminine traits that we find in Olympia, Remedios, Faustine, and La Maga offers us their emblematic nature without letting us into the perspective from which they might be constructing an interpretation and rearrangement of what is give *to them* as experience. María Luisa Bombal has written on such enigmas in much of her fiction. The voices narrating her texts refuse whatever we may recognize as anecdotes; they articulate meanders that take us away from facts. Reality is nevertheless kept there, as a virtuality that does not quite come into being. Thus Bombal's fiction attempts to invent for itself a source of energy that would carry the reader through its pages without an interest in the kinds of events conventionally recognized as plot.

Bombal writes against the grain of the reader's expectations, and as a result her writing suffers from the lack of appeal to reading habits—without losing persuasiveness—that often accompanies experimental works questioning the nature of the representation that makes them possible. The challenge presented by Bombal involves an awareness of the secrets animating her work and the kinds of substitutions that her doll-like stare requires us to perform.

The Uncanniness of Women

She is exactly like her name, thinks Juan Manuel. Pale, angular, and a bit savage. And there is something odd about her that I cannot place. But of course, he realizes as she glides through the door and disappears—her feet are too small. How strange that she can support such a long body on such tiny feet. (p. 88)

This passage from "New Islands"[2] by María Luisa Bombal repeats a ubiquitous preoccupation in her work: the difficulty in adequately defining and portraying a woman. The assymetry between body and feet in Yolanda's appearance provokes a desire to think about her in terms of an assemblage open to analysis and discussion.

What is the mechanism connecting the feet to the rest of the body? And furthermore, how are name and body connected so that their harmony might resolve, at another level, the discomfort caused by the size of the feet? The terms that hold Yolanda's name in continuity with her body are given in a hypothesis that tells us of her closeness to nature. We are told that she is just like her name, "pale, angular and a bit savage."

Yolanda, identical to her name, has an identity beneath or beyond humanity, a name that approximates her to the wilderness, to something not yet conquered. Thus because of her name the lack of knowledge about her as a person acquires the mystery of a natural element. The question regarding the mismatching of feet and body becomes juxtaposed with an essentialist view of that which is symbolized by a name.

It is not only in Yolanda's case that we encounter the enigmas of the wilderness or, in broader terms, nature, invoked in relationship to the definition of a woman's essential being. Bombal's story "The Tree,"[3] included in *New Islands,* tells us about a female character of dubious intelligence named Brígida. Her father, tired after having brought up and educated five older daughters, decides not to do anything about her, leaving her cultural education to her own designs. Brígida is portrayed as the practical product of a kind of semiwildness, in a manner akin to the reflections about Yolanda's name and her body.

Brígida's beauty is eloquently rendered in the story, as well as her capacity to get lost in free association when listening to music. She puzzles the "normal" characters in the story:

> Her eighteen years; her chestnut braids that, unbound, cascaded to her waist; her golden complexion; her dark eyes so wide and questioning. A small mouth with full lips; a sweet smile; and the lightest, most gracious body in the world. Of what was she thinking, seated by the fountain's edge? Of nothing. "She is as silly as she is pretty," they used to say. (pp. 52–53)

Brígida's truth is her innocence, seen as a lack of intelligence or a mere result of ignorance. The story leaves unexplored the "historical" basis for her circumstance; instead, it devotes detailed attention to the excellence of that nothingness in which her thought dwells. Brígida's world is one of music and nature. Her relationship to music is passive, she lets herself go; the link with nature cannot be described so clearly.

Brígida *is* nature in the sense of being unschooled; Luis, her husband, tells her that he married her because of the "scared fawn" look in her eyes. The nights of the imperfect couple are described in vegetable and meteorological terms:

> Unconsciously, he would turn away from her in sleep; just as she unconsciously sought her husband's shoulder all night long, searching for his breath, groping blindly for protection as an enclosed and thirsty plant bends its tendrils toward warmth and moisture. (p. 55)

Brígida's erotic energy is described as a vegetable wish to grow, her being loved as a woman is the result of her resemblance to a frightened animal. The story tells the vulnerability of Brígida's semiwildness in almost caricatured terms. The father who refuses to educate her, the older husband who cannot satisfy her, and everybody else who surrounds her are seen as part of a threatening and foreign humanity.

The story has a happy ending with a resolution that productively engages nature. Brígida *recognizes* herself in a passage in which the evocation of a concert is interspersed with the details of the felling of a rubber tree that used to grow by her window. Brígida had felt that there was a communication between her and the tree when it swayed with the wind. The intensity of her reaction at the felling of the tree is such that the readers understand that they and the characters defined as "normal" are not alone in their inability to grasp Brígida. She had shared in that ignorance and it is only now, through the episode of the tree, that she can finally have access to herself. Her understanding is not the result of analysis. She does not "deal" with her situation; it is in the form of a sudden realization that confirms her unity with nature.

In very much the same way that the tree came down, in one clean and swift moment, Brígida's whole life appears to her as though the result of an illumination:

> She is imprisoned in the web of her past, trapped in the dressing room—which has been invaded by a terrifying white light. It was as if they had ripped the roof; a crude light entering from every direction, seeping through her very pores, burning her with its coldness. And she saw everything bathed in that cold light: Luis, his wrinkled face, his hands crisscrossed with ropy discolored veins, and the gaudy cretonnes. (p. 63)

The awareness is precipitated by the absence of the rubber tree. It is as though her union with Luis had always been dependent on another, more essential coupling: that of Brígida with the rubber tree that preserved through its presence the lie that made life with Luis possible. But what precisely *was* that lie? How can we convey the privileged knowledge that emerges from the disappearance of the rubber tree?

Brígida does not explain her relationship to Luis, she just sees it. Her vision has little to do with the facts that made up her marriage. She leaves the facts aside to present Luis's appearance, the details of his body, his old age. Their home is also seen in its ugliness. Brígida's insights are shown as the result of a sudden change in the way in which she perceives the aesthetic and erotic energy fueling her existence.

Brígida's self-awareness is also a capacity for seeing herself as having been previously incomprehensible. The ugliness of the material elements surrounding her color her sense of her past and, by inference, suggest that from this perception a positive, healing change will emerge.[4] The reader does not know what Brígida's changes will entail, but the story has succeeded in producing an approximation to her initial uncanniness. Even though her character is not specifically explained, the changes she undergoes involve a self-critical move that assimilates her to the reader, allowing her to share our perplexity.

In the remarkable text "The Story of María Griselda,"[5] Bombal gives us a feminine character rich in pre-Raphaelite echoes. The connections between María Griselda and the natural world are drawn in great detail, expanding on the vision of "The Tree" and "New Islands." A whispering, animated, and solidary natural environment is conveyed through associations between events or feelings in María Griselda's life and trees, flowers, horses.

The death of the woman in "Trenzas" is described in conjunction with the reaction of natural elements, reinforcing the sense that there existed a perfect harmony between them:

The doctor assured them that she had agonized throughout the whole night. But the wood had agonized and died with her and her mane of hair sharing in the same roots. (p. 81)

She has been so intertwined with nature that her death changes the natural world, forever inflecting it with what is described as "her magic and wisdom." The loss of the heroine is also the loss of a certain kind of woman; the story ends nostalgically:

And that is why today's women when they undo their braids have lost their seer's powers and have no premonitions, or absurd pleasures, or magnetic power.
  And their dreams are now but a sad tide that brings and takes tired images or one or the other domestic nightmare. (p. 81)

Brígida, Yolanda, and María Griselda are part of a powerful figuration of the relationship between women and nature in Bombal's work. It is not a metaphysics of the eternal feminine applicable to all women. It is, on the contrary, a notation of details that disseminate certain feminine characters in their natural counterparts which, in turn, serve as vehicles for a series of transformations. The hypothesis of the women's link to nature is not enough to explain by itself the uncanniness of Bombal's women. Once it is noted, however, their elusive character turns into a source of complicity between characters and readers.

Desire and Facts

My body and my kisses could not make him tremble but they made him, as before, think about another body and different lips. As he had done years before, I saw him again trying furiously to caress and desire my flesh and always finding the memory of the dead woman between him and me. When he abandoned himself on my breast, his cheek unconsciously would search for the tenderness and contours of another breast. He kissed my hands, he kissed me all over, missing familiar warmths, fragrances, roughnesses. And he cried madly, calling her, screaming to me in my ear absurd things meant for her. (p. 75)

The novel *Final Mist*[6] is about a couple apparently as torn apart as the one in "The Tree." The two are cousins married after the man became a widower. The narrator is the second wife. She describes her sexual encounters with her husband as explorations through which he tries to cancel his first wife's death. The passion that drives him to his second wife stems—according to her—from his faithfulness to an absent body; thus for the narrator making love entails participating in the act as though she were another, giving her body so that it may become a conduit for the unreachable woman. Her participation in sexual intercourse consists of giving testimony of herself as an absence, devoid of identity and allowing her husband's desire to overwhelm her. Being possessed by her husband is also a way of acknowledging his radical rejection of her. Their passion is intensely nostalgic; through it a loss is reactivated, the present is devalued and identities are erased.

The bed where they make love is a theater of representation in which the narrator views her own body as someone else's. Being her husband's wife also means being a different woman. Her own sexual energy is also animated by an object outside her marital relationship. When they make love she feels that she is betraying a lover who has been internalized in her mind as occasioning the most passionate and authentic encounter she had ever had.

One night, to her husband's surprise, the narrator decides to go out for a walk. Daniel, her husband, tells her that it is too late, that she has never gone out alone at such a time. Since it was precisely during such a walk that she recalls having met the man with whom she had the erotic encounter, she insists that she has, indeed, been out that late before. Daniel denies that it happened:

Daniel looks at me straight in the eye for a moment, then asks me mockingly: —"And in your outing did you meet anybody that night"—"A man"—I answer provocatively—"He spoke to you?"—"Yes"—"Do you remember his voice?"

His voice? How was his voice? I don't remember it. Why don't I remember it . . . because I don't know it. I go over each moment of that extraordinary night. I have lied to Daniel. It is not true that the man spoke to me. —"He did not speak to you? You see, he was a ghost." (p. 82)

The humiliation that the narrator feels in her sexual life with her husband is intensified when the existence of her lover is questioned, since her dissatisfaction with her marriage is predicated in contrast to that other privileged experience. Andres, a witness to her encounter with the lover, dies before she can ask him for confirmation of the event.

Because of her experience with the lover she was able to come closer to her husband. Her pleasure, dislodged from the immediate source producing it, became an experience in the second degree, dependent on a nostalgic point of reference. Her desire to be with another man during intercourse with her husband approximated the feelings he had when he longed for the first wife and used the narrator as a vehicle for that end. The possible non-occurrence of the encounter with her lover makes the identification with her husband impossible and, paradoxically, threatens the marriage. The narrator suffers from the loss of the repetitive pleasure of her identifications; she has lost herself as her lover's lover and has never existed as an "original" as her husband's woman.

We should now turn to the quality of the narrator's original experience, whether real or imaginary. What kind of subject was she? To what extent is she free from the chain of proliferations that take her away from holding a univocal identity? The encounter with the man takes place in an anonymous context. We learn about the meeting's consequences in the narrator's mind through a retrospective account, but we also read at the beginning a long passage in the present tense with details about the event. We know that there was a nocturnal walk, a bond without words with a stranger who took the narrator to a house where they made love without talking to each other. The sexual act is described in terms of integration to nature:

> ... then he bends over me and we roll down intertwined to the center of the bed. His body covers me like a big simmering wave, he caresses me, he burns me, he penetrates me, he envelops me, and sweeps me away, fainting. (p. 60)

In her pleasure, the narrator has been nobody. Nameless for her lover, she also forgets her own body so that she may lose it in the current of a sexuality that envelops her and takes her beyond the specificity of the moment. Thus to have been with that man in an experience that colors all others is also to have experienced her oblivion. The present tense of the encounter questions, from its very occurrence, its having taken place. The narrator's best lover is someone who helps her forget who she is. Her participation in the best sexual experience she remembers coincides with a privileged moment of loss of identity, and an entrance into a realm she does not know. The protagonist in *Final Mist*, like Brígida in "The Tree" in relationship to music, longs to be swept away, to forget herself. The voice narrating *Final Mist* suggests that the wife is too full of energy for her husband but exactly matched to her lover, with an energy that is translated into passivity.

Not only does the narrator not know her lover's name, she has also lost her own in the encounter. Two other men represent the poles that could serve as a confirmation of her experience. One is her husband, who doubts she ever took that walk and humiliates her with the suggestion that she remembers a ghost. The other man is a witness who dies before being able to say what he knows. Facing alone the need to grant historicity to the event, the narrator finds in a friend's suicide the opportunity to take the leap that separates her imaginary experience from reality.

On her way to visit an urban hospital she passes the streets she remembers from that night and starts searching for the house where their lovemaking took place. The search is unsuccessful; it produces first a misunderstanding and then another experience of loss of self.

> With the vague hope of having mistaken the street, the house, I keep wandering through the phantasmagoric city. I turn time and again. I would like to keep searching but it is getting dark and I don't see anything. Also, why fight? It was my destiny. The house, my love and my adventure, everything has vanished in the mist; something like a burning hook grips me, suddenly, in the back of my head; I remember I have a fever. (pp. 98–99)

The understanding of her destiny curbs her nostalgia. As in "The Tree," the change is sudden. There is no analytical reworking of the elements of the experience. The reader is asked to reinterpret the novel with the idea that this later walk cancels out the hypothetical one and that the character will again be able to enter a new realm because of an experience in which she is out of control.[7] This time it is not erotic energy that moves her to leave the scenario of her encounter, it is a fever.

The reevaluation of the text taking into consideration its disputed fact (whether the encounter took place or not) is impossible. The narrator fails in her description of herself as subject of her experience, her triumph consists in having delineated the meanders of an itinerary permanently fixed on an elusive past.

Dead Women

A dead woman may be considered a fixed point for narration. With everyday temporal contingencies gone, death produces its own images and becomes a source for signs with a clarity that excludes historical accidents. Voluntary death grants prestige to one of Bombal's feminine characters, Regina, whose suicide is portrayed as an attempt to do away with the mediocre realities with which everyday life is imbued in Bombal's fiction. In *Final Mist* the narrator describes her reaction when she visits Regina in the hospital, where she lies after having attempted to end her life:

> Behind Regina's gesture there is intense feeling, a whole life of passion. Only one recollection supports my life, a recollection whose flame I have to tend every day lest it die. Such a distant and vague recollection that it almost seems to me be a fiction. Regina's disgrace: a wound as a consequence of love, of a true love, of that love made up of years, letters, caresses, tears, resentments, deceit. For the first time I tell myself that I am unhappy, that I have always been horribly and completely unhappy. (p. 93)

Regina's relationship with her lover has the materiality that the narrator lacks. The documentation of the time he and Regina shared and the precipitous end of the relationship open up an interstice through which the novel itself reveals alternatives of texture that it has not fully developed. Regina belongs to an alternative world, where events lead to decisions, where the energy that moves time is made up of "real" facts. For the reader, that reality has a name: it is the conventional novelistic plot.

Regina's death, contemplated by the narrator, is a way of valorizing characters who participate in recognizable situations. Thus the visit to Regina divides the narrative from itself and allows us to perceive the tone in which it is articulated. At the anecdotal level, Regina's suicide allows the narrator to continue the self-pitying discourse that characterizes her. Structurally it offers a view of what the novel has rejected in order to be what it is. In Macedonio Fernández's terms, Regina's story would be a "bad novel."

Without her death, Regina's life is devoid of interest. Because of her death her presence acquires weight and her character comes to life. Dead women interfere in the narrator's erotic life. They are better than she is. Regina and her husband's first wife delineate the referential system against which she measures the extent of her humiliation. It is through Regina that the narrator thinks that her experience with her hypothetical lover was not true love; it is through the first wife that she becomes invisible in her own marriage.

Dead women control the meaning of the relationships that the narrator has with those surrounding her. Her being a woman is rooted in wanting to be a different woman, or be punished with a constant doubt as to who she is. This attraction for dead women, the influence that they have over the narrator, is one of the ways Bombal annotates representation as an unsatisfactory and dark hole, with adventures that might fill it but are denied to her.

Silence

The lack of anecdotal lines, the constant deferment of action, and the nostalgia that permeates occurrences create an atmosphere of stillness in Bombal's work. It is as though the referential aspect of language had been suspended; the characters seem to lack a voice. Like the narrator in *Final Mist* who realizes that her lover had not talked to her only when her husband asks her about what the man had said to her, the reader emerges from the novel incapable of reproducing the voices of the characters that have sustained the fiction.

Nevertheless, there *is* dialogue in Bombal. Her use of language is expressive when the reader is addressed directly, there is an abundant use of exclamation marks, and the punctuation gives the sentences a light, almost colloquial rhythm. The use of dialogue does not ensure, however, that communication occurs under conventional terms. The characters exchange words that expose them without fully integrating them into a narrative texture. The appeals to the reader have the function of conveying the doubts that the narrative voice entertains about itself. The failure of language to convey facts weaves an alternative function for it, in which instead of the illusions of action, we are allowed to have a glimpse at the details of a vast apathetic landscape for the female characters.

Bombal's male characters are vehicles for presenting a dissatisfied female sexuality, in an uneven relationship with husbands and lovers. The ideal is represented by the inactive goal par excellence, death. The character's speech invites the reader into an enclosure where the claustrophobia felt by Bombal's characters is reiterated. The walls of the enclosure are the mediocrity of everyday life, aging, and the lack of love.

The reason speech appears as insufficient is that it implies participation in a world portrayed as worthless. Suffering constitutes a poor response to the limitations of experience, as we read in "The Tree": "Little by little her fever went down as her bare feet grew cold on the reed mat. She did not know why it was so easy to suffer in that room" (p. 64). The enclosures dreamt up by Bombal provide us with a portrait of how the world might be seen from the point of view of a radically antiparticipatory position. The devaluing of the narrator in *Final Mist,* which shows her to be worse than inanimate by telling us that she is invisible because of the peculiar way in which she is inscribed in her relationship to others, becomes even more explicitly delineated in Bombal's novel *La amortajada* (The shrouded woman).[8]

The novel reproduces the perspective of a dead woman watching those around her during her wake. Death is seen as a deliverance from worry and the ravages of age.[9]

And all of a sudden she feels herself without a single wrinkle, pale and beautiful as ever. She is filled with an immense joy, that she should be this admired by those who could only remember her devoured by trivial worries, wilted by some unhappiness and the icy air of the hacienda. Now that they know she is dead, there they all are, surrounding her. (pp. 6–7)

There is a voluptuousness of inaction in *La amortajada* that tells us that death produces pleasure and insight. The strongest passion felt by the dead woman is a continuing hatred for her husband, whose head resting on her breast as he bids his last farewell revolts her. During the novel the dead woman changes her view of her feelings toward her husband as she realizes that she is leaving this world:

No. She does not hate him. But she does not love him either. And it is now, when she stops loving him and hating him, that she senses that the last knot of her vital existence is becoming undone. Nothing matters to her now. It is as though herself and her past had no more reason to be. A great boredom encircles her. Oh, this sudden rebellion! This desire that torments her into getting up, crying: "I want to live. Give it back to me, give me back my hatred!" (p. 78)

The passion that kept her alive was her hatred for her husband. As death installs itself in her consciousness, she realizes that even that energy was worth preserving.

Nathanael saw love in Olympia's sighs and silence, but Bombal's fiction tells us that a woman's silence is the articulation of hatred and resentment; *La amortajada* does not substitute the worthlessness of everyday life with something loftier, more poetic. The dead woman's sense of her past life leads her to speak about María Griselda, who appears in this novel as her daughter-in-law:

Abducted, melancholy, that is how I see you, my sweet daughter-in-law. . . . María Griselda I was the only one capable of loving you. Because I and only I could forgive you so much and such unbelievable beauty. (p. 79)

The relationships among women are the most intense in Bombal's fiction. *Final Mist* offers us the narrator's admiration for Regina and *La amortajada* describes the dead woman's appreciation for María Griselda. The pact sealed among women in Bombal's fiction is not one of political solidarity; it stems, rather, from the notion that women are of vital interest to other women, that the apathetic perception will not be derailed by anecdotes when it focuses on them. Whether they are uncanny like Yolanda, ambiguously related to nature like Brígida, the embodiment of magical beauty like María Griselda, or dead like Regina, it is they who sustain the interest of representation once the naive curiosity for plot has been dismantled. María Luisa Bombal attempts to teach us in great detail that when Olympia's eyes seem to be fixed on Nathanael, they are searching for somebody else, a woman, perhaps María Griselda.

Notes

1. E. T. A. Hoffmann, "The Sandman," in Victor Lange, ed., *Tales* trans. L. J. Kent and E. C. Knight (New York: Continuum, 1982), p. 300.

2. María Luisa Bombal, "New Islands," from her *New Islands and Other Stories,* trans. Richard and Lucía Cunningham (New York: Farrar, Straus, Giroux, 1982). Page numbers are cited according to this edition. The volume includes a preface by Jorge Luis Borges in which he writes, "Today in Santiago,

Chile or Buenos Aires, in Caracas or Lima, when they name the best names, María Luisa Bombal is never missing from the list. This fact is even more notable when one considers the brevity of her work—which does not correspond to any determined 'school' and which fortunately is devoid of any regionalism."

3. María Luisa Bombal, "The Tree," in the cited edition of *New Islands*. Page citations are in accordance with that volume.

4. Some scholars of Bombal's work see in aspects such as these a political statement. According to this view, Bombal would be positing the negative conditions of feminine existence in order to criticize and change society. See María Inés Lagos-Pope, "Silencio y rebeldía: Hacia una valoración de María Luisa Bombal dentro de la tradición de la escritura femenina," in M. Agosín, E. Gascón-Vera, and Joy Renjilian Burgy, eds., *María Luisa Bombal: Apreciaciones críticas* (Tempe, AZ: Bilingual Press, 1987), pp. 119–35, and Mercedes Valdivieso, "Social Denunciation in the Language of 'El Arbol' by María Luisa Bombal," *Latin American Literary Review* 4, 9 (1976): 70–77. Silence, so privileged in Bombal's writing, coupled with death constitute the possibility of an interpretive matrix in which death is seen as the possibility of a retrospective interpretive tool because, as Margaret Higonnet states in an article not dealing specifically with Bombal, "to embrace death is at the same time to read one's life. The act is a self-barred signature; its destructive narcissism seems to some particularly feminine." See Margaret Higonnet, "Speaking Silences: Women's Suicide," in Susan Suleiman, ed., *The Female Body in Western Culture* (Cambridge, MA: Harvard University Press, 1986), p. 69. The explanatory deaths here refer to the characters who are either passive or dead and not to Bombal's own biography.

5. María Luisa Bombal, *La historia de María Griselda* (Valparaíso: Ediciones Universitarias de Valparaíso, 1977). Page citations are according to this edition; my translation. The representation of María Griselda, highly original at the time, has affinities with the literature of Alejandra Pizarnik, whose ubiquitous nostalgia for the figure of a lost young woman "no más las dulces metamorfosis de una niña de seda / sonámbula ahora en la cornisa de niebla" defines her signature as a poet. See Alejandra Pizarnik, *Obras completas* (Buenos Aires: Editorial Corregidor, 1992), p. 69.

6. María Luisa Bombal, *La última niebla* (Buenos Aires: Editorial Andina, 1973). Page citations are according to this edition; my translation. María Luisa Bastos points out the importance of this novel as one of the foundational texts of modern Latin American literature. See María Luisa Bastos, "Escrituras de la ambigüedad," in her *Relecturas* (Buenos Aires: Hachette, 1989), pp. 77–80. The echoes of Bombal's novel are also present in other literatures. Marguerite Duras explores a situation similar to the one in *La última niebla* in *Le ravissement de Lol V. Stein* (Paris: Gallimard, 1964). Like Bombal, she writes a novel to capture the avatars of a female gaze in an episode that mobilizes her sense of self-identity and sexual desire. Violette Leduc's *L'affamée* (Paris: Gallimard, 1948) presents a character with a measure of self-hatred eager to compare herself negatively with others who exhibit Bombal's own refusal to portray female self-satisfaction: "Quand nous arrivons dans un restaurant, je desire la preceder avec la canne du tambour-major. J'appliquerai un loup sur mon visage pour jongler avec cet objet, car je ne veux pas offenser sa beauté avec ma laideur" ("When we arrive in a restaurant my wish is to precede her with the drum-major's baton. I will wear a mask on my face to juggle with that object,

since I don't want to offend its beauty with my ugliness") (p. 93). Susan Suleiman asks: "Who writes or speaks in the 'ne cesse pas, ne cessera pas' that Lacan leaves desiring? Who speaks or writes the ravishment of Lol V. Stein? Feminine discourse, which is not always where one expects to find it, reminds us that when it comes to being human, we are all in a position of ravishment, call it lack, if you must; our only hope for survival—call it love—being, against all odds and through all our divisions, to keep on writing." Susan Suleiman, *Subversive Intent: Gender, Politics and the Avant-Garde* (Cambridge, MA: Harvard University Press, 1990), p. 118. For Bombal, there is no cause for celebration in writing, only a ravishment and its being recorded.

7. For a study of the affinities between Bombal's work and mysticism, see *Las desterradas del paraíso: Protagonistas en María Luisa Bombal* (New York: Senda Nueva Ediciones, 1983). The voluptuousness of pain found in Bombal's writing is understated but pervasive and constitutes an aporetic level of experience, similar to that encountered in more explicitly physical representations of this stand. For an extreme case that takes Bombal's figuration to a most vivid realm, see Jerome Peignot and the group Change, eds., *Ecrits de Laure* (Paris: Pauvert, 1977). Laure acted out in explicit sexual terms the passivity evoked by Bombal.

8. María Luisa Bombal, *La amortajada* (Buenos Aires: Editorial Andina, 1968). Citations are according to this edition; my translation.

9. Naomi Lindstrom examines the peculiarities that the notion of consciousness acquires in *La amortajada* in "El discurso de *Le amortajada*: Convención burguesa vs. conciencia cuestionadora," in Agosín et al., *María Luisa Bombal: Apreciaciones críticas*, pp. 147–61.

Chapter 8
Closing the Book—Dogspeech: José Donoso

Fear and Story-Telling

García Márquez's *Love in the Time of Cholera* offers its French-speaking parrot as a way of parodying the continuation of francophilia with the pleasures of literature. In José Donoso's *A House in the Country*[1] we also encounter the use of French to allude to the puzzles of literary convention, this time in the form of a game called "La marquesa salió a las cinco" played by some characters in the novel; the game's title is a translation of Paul Valéry's much-quoted attack on the novelistic genre.[2] Since *A House in the Country* is not sparing in its use of direct French titles, phrases, and even whole songs, the choice of Spanish for Valéry's phrase rather than its quotation in the original produces an effect of parodical displacement.

A House in the Country focuses on some cousins left by their parents with a group of servants in their wealthy mansion which is surrounded by lands occupied by impoverished natives. In the course of the novel the reader is apprised of the children's anxiety that their parents will not come back from their trip and of the parents' ensuing revulsion toward the situation they face on their return. During the uncertain time between departure and return, the children play "La marquesa salió a las cinco," face diverse dangers, and engage in transgressive sexual practices. The servants rebel only to be kept in place. The carefully fenced mansion is violated as suspicions of cannibalism among natives and other characters contribute to the delineation of a society shaped by greed and brutality. *A House in the Country* is a polytonal work, featuring a straightforward realistic style, a highly allusive and florid mode reminiscent of the turn-of-the century Spanish American "modernistas,"[3] and a playful—at times erudite—use of quotations and foreign terms. The preliminary farewell to the parents initiates the reader into the intricate architecture of the mansion, whose layers hiding gold and family secrets yield, as well, a patchwork of Spanish discursive styles that implicitly constitute another journey, this time into literary tradition.

What are the secrets unveiled during these simultaneous journeys? One concerns the contents of the house library, a room filled with richly bound volumes, which is off limits to the children and in which Adriano Gomara, the unfortunate father of one of the cousins, is being held prisoner by the rest of the family. Arabela, the keeper of the room, is a cousin thought by all to possess an unusual degree of information. When cousin Wenceslao, a boy whose mother enjoys dressing him up as a girl, is told by Arabela that the library contains nothing but empty bindings made to order by their grandfather for the sake of appearances, he ponders in shock the source of Arabela's knowledge because he realizes that it could not be traced to her studying in the library, as he had originally thought.

> How does she know so much? The answer in his head took the form of a stampede of other immediate questions: but is it true that she knows so much? Or do I only think so because I know so little myself, and do the grown-ups only think so when they go to consult her because it suits their purposes that she should? (p. 17)

The narrator reassures us that the grown-ups had known all along that only bindings filled the four-story salon called "the library" and that the interdiction denying the children access to that room (issued on the pretext of protecting their eyesight from stress and their minds from being misguided) was, in fact, another exercise of the parents' persistent wish to domesticate their offspring by having them follow orders.

Arabela's knowledge becomes linked to books, only to underscore the point that the alleged source of her information is sheer make-believe. Once the hypothesis of her familiarity with the library's authors and languages is dismissed, she becomes all the more puzzling to Wenceslao and the reader because Arabela is made to embody a knowledge *around* reading, but without any source *in* reading. Her wisdom stems in large measure from her recognition that nothing can be found in that library. Arabela is superior to her cousins because she is unaffected by the authority of the contents of library shelves. She is also familiar with the pain of Adriano Gomara, whose screams are heard when he is not drugged or asleep. Made indifferent to Adriano's pain because of the frequency of his protests and cynical about what might be learned from reading books, Arabela laughs at Wenceslao's bewilderment. In this early scene of the novel, Wenceslao's emotion in finding his father and his realization that the library is fake are presented in counterpoint to Arabela's allowing the question about how she attains knowledge to be addressed. Is her knowledge a hypothesis—as Wenceslao thinks—needed by both children and grown-ups? Or is it something firmer, grounded untransferably in Arabela?

If in *Love in the Time of Cholera* Fermina's superior intuition generated the energy needed to put the book aside and engage in "life," Arabela's strength in *A House in the Country* lies in a different domain.[4] She laughs. Her laughter *against* the sentimentality attendant in Wenceslao's reunion with his father and the shock of her revelation about the library destroys the possibility of investing them with anything but detachment. Arabela's laughter empties this part of the novel of the feelings she derides. Thus although she implies (like Fermina) that the realm of books is to be left for something else, her pursuit of that other realm has the vertiginous nature of destructive humor rather than the safer, canonized trappings of love associated with Fermina.

Cruel laughter superimposed onto a basic and unredeemable fear, not love, is the grounding reality presented by *A House in the Country* as the "other" of literature capable of telling us about the emptiness of the bindings in the library. Is Arabela's message right? Are there not books in the library? Or, in other words, how *different* are the occurrences that make up the novel from those encountered in reading literature?

The game "La marquesa salió a las cinco," played without explicit reference to the original French, is a key to some of the answers provided by the novel. Organized by a cousin named Juvenal, whose imprecations to the rest of the children are reminiscent of the Roman satirist,[5] the children change roles and engage in a form of play-acting that soon causes them to blur the distinction between the game's make-believe and that other layer perceived in the novel as their reality: a reality forceful enough to generate a baby born of one of the couplings between cousins even though, according to the temporal frame of the novel, such an event would have been impossible. In opposition to Valéry's disparaging dictum about the genre of the novel, fiction unravels without recourse to pedestrian commonsensical statements. The upsetting of time generated by "La marquesa salió a las cinco" within the novel is a forceful denial of the implications of "La marquise est sortie à cinq heures."

Love in the Time of Cholera's Dr. Urbino died trying to catch a parrot that he had tried to teach French; his last words, "ca y est," are to be completed—the reader intuits—by his playful executioner in a combination of verbal obedience and creole triumph at having gotten rid of the cumbersome teacher, ca y est. In shifting "La marquise est sortie à cinq heures" to the active game of "La marquesa salió a las cinco," *A House in the Country* grounds literature in the humor of displacement.

There may not be books in that library and, indeed, there is contempt for those who would flow toward them in search of a wisdom better found elsewhere. The entanglements and occurrences among characters are suggested as the best realization of what is merely hinted at in books.

The relationship between literature and life is doubly registered in *A House in the Country*. On the one hand, the children's game creates a level of fiction within fiction with limits blurred by the hypothesis of the birth of a "real" baby, echoing the expected birth in Donoso's novel *The Obscene Bird of Night*.[6] On the other hand, a narrator with a will to control and intervene in the creation of the plot frames this layer with his comments and even a casual encounter in the street with one of the family members portrayed in the book who refuses his account as fanciful and boring. The story we read has not been well told, he says. The effect, as in García Márquez's *One Hundred Years of Solitude,* is to make us think that we should reread the whole novel with a critical eye. Yet whereas in García Márquez we would effectively void the history of the family through the hypothetical reinterpretation triggered by the rereading, in *A House in the Country* the perspective of the Ventura family member encountered in the street produces a different effect. His view dims both the horror and the wealth housed in the mansion. Without its sharp edges, the story turns, as if in a moment of "La marquesa salió a las cinco," into an insipid narrative—Valéry's and, of course, Donoso's refused alternative. Fear becomes paradoxically recognized as essential to the interest in the characters and the pleasure of the reception of their story.

As Seen by a Hungry Dog

Is *A House in the Country* to be understood, then, as the rather bland but effective reinstatement of a narrator capable of undermining Valéry's condescension to novelistic efforts? Donoso's book offers a larger enclosure in this regard, one that renders the frictions between art and life in a different and more eloquent register.

Tapestries and paintings abound in the tale. Unlike books they hold clues to the interpretation of events to come and are regarded as important elements in the visual and interpretative matrix of the reading. Such is the case, for example, of the wall-hanging "L'embarquement pour Cythère"[7] that is described as the parents are planning their departure. If a painting or tapestry anticipates and in so doing *participates* in shaping an event, can it not be said that this visual object exercises control over the events outside its representation? One of the servants, Juan Pérez, undertakes the task of restoring a tapestry hanging in the mansion. As he is portrayed performing the work, it becomes immediately apparent that the fresco trompe l'oeil has the capacity to perceive. It is no mere adornment:

> This eye, muttered Juan Pérez—dipping his brush in sea-green glitter and dotting the pupil of the greyhound, which stood peering into the ballroom through a door he had pawed open—will be my eye. It will take in everything: when I am not around, it will be here to spy on them. (p. 227)

In restoring the trompe l'oeil, Juan Pérez renders a version of it that upsets the social order that distributes roles in the represented scene. The greyhound is neither a domestic pet nor a well-trained hunting dog; furthermore, Juan Pérez himself refuses to be the courtier in the picture and, instead, makes himself one with the dog's eye:

> But he wished to make it quite clear that he wasn't that courtier, he was this famished greyhound whose black ribs he was now accentuating with shadows. Everything he restored with his brush seemed to turn into a hallucinated freak. His henchmen, dangling on scaffolds and pulleys at various heights over the face of the fresco, were busy imperceptibly transforming the frolicsome goddesses into harpies, the rosy clouds into thunderheads. This dog would see with a detail as sharp as its hunger everything Juan Pérez couldn't see for himself, what with his nose stuck inches from the wall, surrounded by paint pots, his back to the room. (pp. 227–28)

Juan Pérez is the dog's eye; the dog's eye is Juan Pérez, but the dog sees more than Juan Pérez does in spite of being a product of his restoration. The dog stands guard in the fresco and redeems Juan Pérez of his subservient role in the family. Its frightening and famished stare forever keeps score.

The dog's hungry stare seems to move the brush restoring the fresco, turning the participants in the scene into hallucinated freaks. What have they seen to look that way? It is not what they see but the manner in which they are stared at. With no more room for frolicking framed by harmonious relationships of power and subservience, the dog has uncovered the capacity underlying the scene. The dog watches hungrily, framing what it perceives with the tendentiousness of its hatred; its gaze transforms. At war with its object of attention, it imposes a paralyzing watch. It is not attacking anybody, though; it is, most important, setting a tone for the scene and uncovering the nature of its elements.

Arabela spoke to the emptiness of the library and laughed off Adriano Gomara's pain. The dog—beyond words—is to complete the lessons of her humor, taking them one step further toward the representation of the social order of the house in the key of a famished stare.

Not books but a fresco trompe l'oeil tells us, again, that what matters is something other, more weighty, than whatever is found in bound volumes. Do we dare call it "life"? The half-alive characters who mingle with the inhabitants of the fresco do not assert a stark opposition between art and life. On the contrary, they posit a deeper understanding of art that would permeate our interpretation of life.

We encounter a dog that has become silent narrator and reweaver of the tale in Donoso's *La misteriosa desaparición de la marquesita de Loria*.[8] This short novel starts out as a playful, early twentieth-century erotic tale. A young woman brought up in strict convent fashion is married and loses her husband soon afterward. Her widowhood is an initiation into intense and transgressive sexual pleasures. The atmosphere in which Blanca, the young woman who becomes the Marquise of Loria, lives is one of detailed luxury. The decor of her house is described at length, recalling the fascination of turn-of-the-century modernistas for the literary rendition of ornamental objects.

The harmony of the marquise's world is upset by an amorous relationship with a man who has a dog named Luna—"moon" in Spanish. Blanca's link to the dog is strong and unquestionable; a physical bond is forged from the beginning, so that when we read of Blanca's reaction upon encountering the dog in her house, we are not surprised:

As she opened the door of her darkened bedroom she felt that her heart leaped in shock, leaving her breathless: there were those two eyes like two moons swimming in that infinite warm, dark, and aromatic space. She perceived a new horizon of potent primitive and essential smells. She did not turn on the lights. The eyes approached her slowly in the dark until she saw the bottom of the hollow pupils, the other side of those eyes whose iridescence came out in drops of saliva from the growling dog. With a growl suddenly become louder Luna launched itself over her, throwing her onto the floor on top of the shards of crystal, slapping her with its rough legs, taking her clothes off again with its hot body, biting her as though it were about to swallow up her satined body, her perfect breasts. . . .
There they were, those two limpid eyes, like two blank continents, like two sheets of paper without any writing. (pp. 162–63)

Blanca is released by the dog, we are told, when "it realizes that she was dissolving herself in the first spasm of the night." The implication is that Blanca felt a voluptuous pleasure in having been ravished. The next morning Blanca looks at her battered body and, after hearing the sounds of the dog next door and seeing it later outside her window, decides not to tell anyone what happened. She breaks up with one of her suitors because "she suffered such boredom when she saw his black imploring eyes which lacked the essential" (p. 168) and devotes herself to a secret life of acknowledging her relationship with Luna.

Blanca (white) is the epithet for Luna (moon). The bond between Luna and Blanca acquires the necessity of a noun and its epithet. Luna's destruction of Blanca's modernista context and its slide into shards and ruins is hyperbolized in Blanca's end. She disappears mysteriously after taking a ride with a man with whom she has sex. Accused of killing her, he defends himself from the charges by saying that she had been taken away by a huge animal, in the middle of the night. Although the man is incarcerated, accused of a crime of passion, the reader—sharing the secret about the bond joining Blanca and Luna—knows that his being put away does not solve the puzzle of the violence that swallowed up Blanca.

After seeing and being stared at by the emptiness at the bottom of Luna's eyes, Blanca cannot but have her ornamental context dismantled. She gives herself away to be ravished by the dog's hungry, revealing eyes. *La misteriosa desaparición de la marquesita de Loria* goes one step beyond in the articulation of the consequences of the dog's watch. Whereas the greyhound restored by Juan Pérez is merely keeping guard, Luna becomes the privileged dismantler of useless ornament, the supreme ravisher, capable of revealing to Blanca the pain at the core of the pleasure precipitating her into their bond. Blanca and Luna, adjective and noun, also suggest a threat to the reader being watched every night by the white moon, "la blanca luna."

A Beautiful Face, Great Clothes

Blanca's ornamental world, her furniture, clothes, and accessories, are destroyed by the emptiness of the dog's fury. The uncertainty about the "true" existence of the dog renders the impact of its destructive energy in a most disturbing form. The hypothesis of its existence being lodged within Blanca, rather than in an external form, incorporates the threat as an inescapable realization of the emptiness of the self. Blanca, white, is just an adjective for Luna, moon—the uncontrollable dark hole driving her into pleasure and final obliteration. As an epithet inextricably attached to her noun, the truth for Blanca is the realization of her annihilation.

The traces left by Blanca are "a silver brooch of her *cloche,* one French shoe, and her golden *Patek Philippe*" (p. 194). The fragments of objects she has bought are retrieved as the only signs of her hypothetical uniqueness. Blanca's manufacturing of her persona through the acquisition of things is part of a sustained figuration of the self in contemporary society elucidated in Donoso's works. One of the novellas in the volume *Tres novelitas burguesas*[9] (three novellas of the middle class)—translated into English as *Sacred Families* in a rendition that conveys the sarcasm of the original title but forgoes its emphasis on compulsive consumption—offers one of the most intense figurations of the disturbing nature of fashion in our society.

"Chatanooga Choochoo" introduces us to the lives of a group of well-to-do characters, frequent consumers of culture and objects. Among them is Sylvia, a model with a "perfect face" whose features have to be literally drawn for every photo opportunity. What was an intimation of emptiness for Blanca is a celebration of possibilities and profit for Sylvia:

> The feeling that Sylvia—that woman-adjective, woman decoration, that collapsible, foldable woman who represented all comforts of modern life and lacked everything, even individuality and togetherness—had magical powers and was therefore powerful, must have dominated my sleep. I could only remember fragments of my dreams, not capture them whole, and I woke up fearing Sylvia. The first thing I felt on opening my eyes was an uncontrollable urge to see her again. What face was she wearing today? What dress did she have on, she who depended so much on clothes? A scarf knotted a certain way could change her whole appearance, not just physically, but inside, as a person. . . . I desired her . . . I definitely wanted to continue my "affair" with her; but more urgent than that, or perhaps what gave strength and shape to that urgency, was the need to erase her face with vanishing cream and throw myself into the delight of painting her and making her up again. (pp. 46–47)

Dancing with her friend Magdalena to the tune of "Chattanooga Choochoo" at a party, Sylvia suggests a disconcerting twinhood. She who can be made up to look like anybody could also *be* at the bottom of everybody. Huidobro's eloquent celebration of the permanent nostalgia inflicted by the intense love for a woman, "Todas las mujeres se te parecen / ahora que no te pareces a ninguna"[10] (All women resemble you / now that you don't resemble anyone), is repeated in a darkly humorous mode. The narrator's attraction to Sylvia draws him to the void, suggests to him the possibility of an ultimate empowerment: being able to efface and make up a new face for her.

Vanishing cream and makeup are to be understood both in their literal meanings and as objects of consumption. Sylvia is the supreme cosmetic product in the novel, ideally faceless and manageable and, because of it, a promise of perfect beauty with each new product. Magdalena, the narrator's wife, has a face of her own but needs to fight its wish to come out from under the makeup, so that she can be the face on the magazine covers like Sylvia. In a scene referred to by the narrator as a "surrogate of lovemaking" (p. 50), he makes up Magdalena.

Making up Magdalena is rendered as a kind of initiation of the narrator into something that is simultaneously new and necessary; he does it naturally as if he were meant for the role. The exercise also brings back to him scenes from his childhood, important recollections that shaped his sense of who he was. The narrator is not involved in a mindless game; he has invested himself totally in an experience with the revelatory powers of love:

> It was a game, masquerade and mask . . . and I thought about my childhood, when in summer homes in the hills we would invent costumes, stick our heads inside transparent silk stockings that preserved our individual features while disguising them; on them we would paint other faces, the bad man's grim scowl, the princess's white, chaste face, the witch's mean beak, the old hag's wrinkles, the patriarch's moustache and beard—but always with our features preserved under the false, transparent skin of the silk stockings. Thus with Magdalena now, who wasn't Magdalena but a mutation of the Sylvia mask, and these in turn were every possible variation of the mythological faces that appeared in fashion magazines which in turn were infinite variations of a mask created by some makeup artist in collaboration with a manufacturer. (p. 51)

Magdalena is able to approach Sylvia's look as though she were covering her face with a silk stocking. One snag and her own features might upset the perfection of the makeup. Attaining Sylvia's look is the opposite of copying from an original deemed to be more authentic, grounded more deeply into existence than its imitation. Magdalena does not have the blank-page face of Sylvia. Had she been faceless like her she would have been able to possess any face she wanted.

Magdalena being made up by her husband is a parody of the transforming powers of love. His pleasure in achieving the appearance he wants her to have suggests that the identification with fragments of representation provided by advertising and art is all we have for articulating the terms of our desire. But "Chatanooga Choochoo" does not present us an ideal couple with the compliant wife ready to follow, in a world of high consumption, the whims of her husband. The voluptuousness of the narrator's sexual encounter with Sylvia conveys the desperation of his will to dominate women. Sylvia, her head shaped like an egg, does not have a face when she is not wearing makeup; she cannot speak because she is mouthless. This state generates great tenderness in the narrator, who sees her as an ideal woman. When he feels like it, he follows her to the bathroom and cuts out a mouth for her in lipstick with the same ease with which he had made up Magdalena. It is as though he were perfecting a kind of lovemaking, delving further into implications of a privileged coupling. The first thing Sylvia does after the narrator creates a mouth on her face is sing "Chattanooga Choochoo." Then she kisses him:

> Abruptly she fell silent and, coming closer, she put her newly cut out mouth on mine and kissed me. Unable to resist the impulse, I took her in my arms and

that kiss—which undoubtedly she had given me to test the effectiveness of her mouth in all its functions—made me experience the ultimate satisfaction of kissing and perhaps even of loving a woman who is not complete: the power of civilized man, who does not cut out tongues or put out chastity belts—primitive procedures—but who knows how to compel a woman's submission by removing or putting on her mouth, taking her apart by removing her arms, her hair in the form of a wig, her eyes in the form of false eyelashes, eyebrows, blue shadow on the lids, removing, by means of some curious mechanism, her sex itself, so she can only use it when he needs her, so that her entire being depends on a man's will—singing or not singing "Chattanooga Choochoo." (p. 27)

Bioy Casares's *Asleep in the Sun*[11] renders a phantasy in its nightmarish resolution by having the man who institutionalizes his wife so that her soul may be transplanted for a dog's become the victim of exchanges he naively thought were under his control. His notion of ideal love is not to be realized in spite of the "scientific" means attempted to bring it into existence. Similarly, the will for total control in "Chatanooga Choochoo" makes a victim of the one who wants to exercise it. Sylvia and Magdalena watch the narrator and Ramon, Sylvia's husband, dressed in identical suits sing and move to the beat of "Chattanooga Choochoo" for them. The transformations affecting Sylvia and Magdalena are infectious; the men are also subjected to the submissive powers represented by the song. It is a minor song and the elements causing the submission are not part of a sinister culture of sexual dominance. They are, instead, the everyday gestures, perceptions, objects, and sounds that mold men and women.

Swept away by the monster Luna, Blanca in *La misteriosa desaparición de la marquesita de Loria* embodies desire as a self-destructive conundrum; her watch as *blanca luna*—white moon—over the characters in "Chatanooga Choochoo" uncovers the possibility of a more sinister and unavoidable emptiness with the same power as Luna's, this time embodied in the faceless stare of the lover in our dreams.

A Greyhound, a Yellow Dog, and Despair

Donoso's *La desesperanza*[12] (Hopelessness), translated into English as *Curfew,* was published in 1986 and, unlike his other works, deals explicitly with a political situation. Two characters, Mañungo and Judit, are stranded in the streets of Santiago de Chile after the curfew established by the military regime. If found out, their lives would be in jeopardy. The novel describes the events of that night in a straightforward manner, emphasizing the cruelty of the political conditions endured by the country at large.

Dogs are again a key to the understanding of what is at stake in the narrative. As Mañungo and Judit look for shelter in the deserted streets, Judit sees a group of rough male dogs in pursuit of a delicate looking small female dog. They run after her, succeeding at points in cornering her with the visible desire to violate her. The peril faced by the female dog is told from a perspective that, in humanizing her, makes her situation applicable to the one experienced by Judit. As in Cortázar's "Press Clippings" the scene of nocturnal violence acquires a claustrophobic generality.

> At a corner, they saw the pack of dogs on the opposite side of the street. The enormous, maddened dog, and underneath him, between his paws, with her fur sticking to her nakedness, the little white bitch waited, licking her chops, while the beast satisfied his trivial impulse. The other dogs formed a querulous and expectant circle around the male, who could not seem to mount the bitch to his satisfaction. As soon as she saw the little white dog, Judit pulled away from Mañungo, crossed the street oblivious of who might see or hear her, and shouted scat, leave her alone, pardon her. But the dogs were unwilling to leave the bitch, whose eyes seemed even more deeply shadowed and decadent, her face more concentrated and pale, accepting that all dogs wanted to possess her. [. . .] Mañungo, just outside the circle, shouted to Judit to get away, to let the disgusting dogs do what they wanted. The dogs jumped around Judit, tearing her sleeves, her skirt, her blouse, staining her with their saliva, with their semen, with their blood, ready to rape her. (p. 181)

Mañungo is outside the circle made by the dogs, echoing the position he has in Chilean political life because he has just arrived from Paris. Judit, inside the circle, suffers the dog's threat from within, as though her own destiny were intertwined with the fate of the pursuit.

The small female dog, having decided to submit to the pack's attack, is playing a survival game. She is the acquiescent victim in a dark apprenticeship imposed by the rule of force. But Judit interferes with her decision, she stands in the circle in an attempt to defend her. Suddenly Judit, who is holding a pistol, decides to use it.

> She aimed at the dogs. There were so many. All the same. All of them deserved to die, undifferentiated males sticking to her and sullying her. In the middle of the pack was the little white bitch, poised as if all this were taking place in a salon, revealing the effect of this fury unleashed by her situation only in her melancholy smile, as if she knew that while she couldn't escape her destiny, she could at least play. Judit did not reach the bitch because the dogs were biting her streaming legs. She was a yard away from her. Between them the seething mob heaved. It seemed that the little white dog was not upset, because from between the paws of the tan dog in the center of the infernal circle, tender, clean, tired, she smiled at Judit, her accomplice, her savior, her sister, who aimed the pistol and shot her in the head. The body twitched and the bitch fell dead. (pp. 181–82)

The result of Judit's intervention in the conflict is the destruction of the small female dog's strategy for survival. Judit's solidarity with her has effectively denied her life and shown to Judit the uncertainty governing any effort to overcome violence. This scene stands as the best rendition of what the original Spanish title of the novel conveys, a hopelessness so pervasive that every effort to stop aggression turns into its opposite. The compliant victim, having understood the message delivered by the drooling pack, had opted for expanding the powers of the pack even further; Judit by executing her turned her into an unwilling martyr to an unstated cause.

Did the dog die in dignity? Or was her acquiescence enough to make her a member of the attacking pack? Cortázar's Noemí ("Press Clippings") and Puig's Molina (*The Kiss of the Spider Woman*) attempt to enter the realm in which all this may be explained; for Donoso certain games hold a key to the answer. They are not, as in Cortázar's *Hopscotch*, preexisting games reinscribed through writing but, as in "La marquesa salió a las cinco," invented ones that serve to uncover as conventional what we think of as belonging to the nature of society.

The Obscene Bird of Night, a somber novel narrated by a character alternatively called Humberto Peñaloza or "El Mudito" (the mute), is the starting point for many of the figurations found in Donoso's later works. As in *A House in the Country*, a large architectural enclosure, this time a convent, serves as the theater for the occurrences in the novel. Masks and lovemaking are brought together, questioning the stability of the self, and a meditation about clothing and rags anticipates the poetics of self-destruction that shapes *La misteriosa desaparición de la marquesita de Loria*, "Átomo verde número cinco," as well as the novellas gathered in *Cuatro para Delfina*.[13]

A yellow female dog is mentioned in *The Obscene Bird of Night* as the witness of an unspeakable secret that joins a little girl, her father, and an old woman who is presented simultaneously as a nanny and a witch. The dog appears at key moments in the narrative as two characters make sexual contact but interrupt it, fearing the dog's gaze. The yellow dog, silent but capable of running away with a secret held by its stare, closes the novel when a group of toothless old women play a game called "la perra amarilla" (yellow bitch). Betting everything they have, these old women, portrayed as indistinguishable and hence anonymous, lose their dentures, the contents of their newspaper-wrapped packages, and, by implication, whatever may be understood as making up their lives.

The newspapers, which reproduce the events of the day, are also disseminated in the game thanks to the randomness of who wins and who loses. Every loss or win is illusory, though, because we are told that in the end the only winner is the yellow bitch, "la perra amarilla." The dog says nothing as it runs away, obliterating history as represented by the old newspapers and erasing the individuality of the old women by taking everything from them. It is a total sweep; the dog is the supreme and uninvited player.

Should we make the dog say its message? Is there a moral that could make its way through the dog and represent us, our point of view? "La perra amarilla," like the other dogs in Donoso's stories, is not there so that we may speak through her in a triumph of domestication. These dogs already exist beyond the ambiguity of Kafka's animal as quoted by Borges;[14] they have won the staring battle and will not be vehicles for a message. On the contrary, as they stand in paralyzing guard they dare us to articulate their silence and learn the lesson they already hungrily know about us.

Notes

1. José Donoso, *Casa de campo* (Madrid: Seix Barral, 1978); trans. David Pritchard with Suzanne Jill Levine, *A House in the Country* (New York: Vintage Books, 1984). Page numbers correspond to the English translation; in some cases I have modified the translation for accuracy.

2. I am indebted to Michel Rybalka, from Washington University in St. Louis, for the information on the probable source for this Valéry quotation: it appears cited by Breton in the second Surrealist manifesto. See André Breton. "Second manifeste du surréalisme" (Paris: Sagittaire, 1929).

3. I refer to the school led by Ruben Darío. Donoso's novel takes up some of this modernista's favorite motifs and reinscribes them in a sinister key. See, for example, the treatment of gold in the chapter bearing that title ("El Oro") (pp. 166–200). The continued references to power and the materiality of its objects in Donoso's fiction have led to more than one interpretation favoring analysis of ideologies. See, for example, Hugo Achúgar, *Ideología y estructuras narrativas en José Donoso* (Caracas: Centro de Estudios Rómulo Gallegos, 1979), and Ricardo Gutiérrez Mouat, "El desclasamiento como ideología y forma en la narrativa de José Donoso," in his *El espacio de la crítica* (Madrid: Orígenes, 1989).

4. Arabela's knowledge gives her a peculiar kind of power, attained in some of Donoso's other works by old women, as in *The Obscene Bird of Night*, or derelicts, as in "Gaspar de la Nuit."

5. The vaguely archaic names of the cousins, clashing with the more "modern" references in the text, reinforce the sense that part of the narrative is to be construed as transhistorical. The role Juvenal plays in building this effect is important, having developed a narrative strategy seen by some as characteristic of postmodernism. John Barth has noted Donoso's relationship to postmodernism in "Post-Modernism Revisited," *Review of Contemporary Fiction* 8 (Fall 1988): 16–24.

6. José Donoso, *El obsceno pájaro de la noche* (Madrid: Seix Barral, 1970).

7. The wall-hanging is also an allusion to Charles Baudelaire's "Un voyage à

Cythère." The joint consideration of the wall-hanging and the poem delineate the deterioration and sorrow to take place in the novel. The final lines of the poem, "Ah! Seigneur! donnez moi la force et le courage / De contempler mon coeur et mon corps sans dégoût!" uncannily encapsulate the characters' final despair. See Charles Baudelaire, "Un voyage à Cythère," *Les fleurs du mal,* in *Oeuvres complètes* (Paris: Bibliothèque de la Pléiade, 1961), pp. 111–13.

8. José Donoso, *La misteriosa desaparición de la marquesita de Loria* (Barcelona: Seix Barral, 1981). Page numbers are in accordance with this edition; my translation. See also Philip Swanson, "Structure and Meaning in *La misteriosa desaparición de la marquesita de Loria,*" *Bulletin of Hispanic Studies* 3 (July 1986): 247–56.

9. José Donoso, *Tres novelitas burguesas* (Barcelona: Seix Barral, 1973), trans. Andree Conrad, *Sacred Families* (New York: Knopf, 1977). Page numbers refer to the English edition.

10. See Vicente Huidobro, "Altazor," in his *Obras completas* (Santiago: Editorial Zig Zag, 1976).

11. See Chapter 5 herein, devoted to Adolfo Bioy Casares.

12. José Donoso, *La desesperanza* (Barcelona: Seix Barral, 1986), trans. Alfred MacAdam, *Curfew* (New York: Weidenfeld and Nicolson, 1988); quotations and page numbers are in accordance with the English translation.

13. José Donoso, *Cuatro para Delfina* (Barcelona: Seix Barral, 1982).

14. See the epigraph for Chapter 2.

Chapter 9
Overstaying My Welcome: Conclusions

What, then, has been dreamt throughout this book as "pedagogical?" What are the constraints of this old term, revived yet eroded by the condescension of the century's consensus? They are certainly not a single body of learned truths but the production of effects of truth and lucidity through fiction. Macedonio's role as a precursor and master of Jorge Luis Borges counters the conventional wisdom that situates Borges's work within the antimetaphysical perspectives of deconstruction, by showing the way his concerns are tied to Macedonio's metaphysical literature. The emergence of the theory of reading explored in the chapter devoted to Macedonio becomes for Borges in our interpretation a meditation about historical repetition intertwined with perplexities about ethics. What Macedonio believed beyond a doubt—that literature could teach—is for Borges material for both humor and serious reflection.

Macedonio Fernández and Borges present models of literature as a form of understanding in which intuition and discursive intelligence are seen as alternately complicitous and conflicting. The readings of their works in the first two chapters set the epistemological groundwork to understand how in the case of García Márquez (in the third chapter) intuition is favored as a means both of attaining knowledge and of transmitting it. "Literature as Risk: Julio Cortázar" takes up the challenge posed by the previous chapters and casts the question in terms of Cortázar's writing: assuming that it is in the nature of literature to become fully realized only through an active reading, what would be the characteristics of a piece of fiction that would truly and practically incorporate in its texture the unfinished quality implied by the act of writing? What and for whom are its lessons? The reading of *Hopscotch,* by highlighting the importance of the more naturalistic moments of the novel, questions its previous interpretations. Cortázar privileges the city and a postsurrealist notion of necessary encounters among his characters and between reader and author as the basis for incorporating whatever knowledge is to be elicited from fiction. Adolfo Bioy Casares, in Chapter 5, is shown to question such an approach. His links with Borges and Macedonio are brought into focus as a framework for understanding character definition in the post-experimental fictions of our period and the pedagogical imperative entailed in his recasting characters and plots from fables and mythology. Love, in the process, becomes a misadventure in which two levels of representation either clash or are indifferent to one another.

The question about gender and knowledge in the context of the pedagogical is unfolded in the readings of Puig and Bombal. Are there forms of knowledge that stem from the misencounter between the genders? In reading Puig we see how the issues discussed in the previous chapters are transferred from literature to popular culture and how the transmission of knowledge becomes engulfed in considerations of style and gender, opening up a meditation about the ultimate pessimism with which postmodern discourses view the production of meaning. Through Bombal the links between the Hoffmannesque tradition of the fantastic and the motifs of silence, passivity, and privileged forms of understanding are highlighted as an alternative way of thinking about the role of literature. "Closing the Book: Dogspeech, José Donoso" implicitly revives the motifs presented previously and weaves them into his work. Whereas the first chapter dealt with Macedonio Fernández, whose extreme optimism about the pedagogical nature of literature led him to believe that its exercise would grant immortality to its readers, the last chapter engages a desperate vision in which language is seen leading to a dark hole. The pedagogical, through the motif of the dogs, is shown as the ultimate impossibility.

To teach, to tell aporetically or with confidence in style, to write and revolutionize, to pose as being dead already, to joke about history and be puzzled by the ubiquity of its repetitions—the register I have composed in this book speaks of the risks of fiction and its worth, its play at being both counterfeit and true.

Since Macedonio found it hard to believe that his readers would proceed through his *Museum of the Novel of the Eternal* sequentially and having read each of his pages, he offered summaries dedicated to those who would not have the patience of accompanying him word by word. An ultimate pedagogical gesture, imitated here not without an awareness of the manner with which we have learned to receive any recasting.

Bibliography

Achúgar, Hugo. *Ideología y estructuras narrativas en José Donoso.* Caracas: Centro de Estudios Rómulo Gallegos, 1979.
Alazraki, Jaime, ed. *Jorge Luis Borges.* Madrid: Taurus, 1976.
Alexandrian, Sarane. *Hans Bellmer.* New York: Rizzoli, 1972.
Andreu, Jean. "Personnage, lecteur, auteur." *L'Arc* 80 (1981): 24–34.
Bacarisse, Pamela. *The Necessary Dream: A Study of the Novels of Manuel Puig.* Totowa, NJ: Barnes and Noble, 1988.
Barrenechea, Ana María. *La expresión de la irrealidad en la obra de Jorge Luis Borges.* México: Colegio de México, 1957.
———. "Horacio en el proceso de escritura de *Rayeula*: Pretexto y texto." *Sur* 350–51 (1982): 45–63. (Buenos Aires)
Barth, John. "Post-Modernism Revisited." *Review of Contemporary Fiction* 8 (Fall 1988): 16–24.
Bastos, María Luisa. *Relecturas: Estudios de textos hispanoamericanos.* Buenos Aires: Hachette, 1989.
Baudelaire, Charles. *Les fleurs du mal.* In *Oeuvres complètes.* Paris: Bibliothèque de la Pléiade, 1961.
Bioy Casares, Adolfo. *La aventura de un fotógrafo en La Plata.* Buenos Aires: Emecé, 1985.
———. *Dormir al sol.* Buenos Aires: Emecé, 1973. Translation by Suzanne Jill Levine, *Asleep in the Sun.* New York: Persea Books, 1978.
———. *El héroe de las mujeres.* Madrid: Alfaguara, 1979.
———. *La invención de Morel.* Buenos Aires: Losada, 1940. Translation by Ruth L. Simms, *The Invention of Morel and Other Stories.* Austin: University of Texas Press, 1985.
———. *Una muñeca rusa.* Barcelona: Tusquets, 1991.
———. *Plan de evasión.* Buenos Aires: Galerna, 1969; Barcelona: EDHASA, 1990. Translation by S. J. Levine, *A Plan for Escape,* New York: Gray Wolf, 1988.
Blanqui, Louis Auguste. *Instructions pour une prise d'armes: L'éternité par les astres et autres textes.* Paris: Société Encyclopédique Française et Éditions de la Tête de Feuilles, 1972.
Bloom, Harold, ed. *Jorge Luis Borges.* New York: Chelsea House, 1986.
Bombal, María Luisa. *La amortajada.* Santiago: Nascimento, 1941; Buenos Aires: Editorial Andina, 1968.

———. *La historia de María Griselda*. Valparaiso: Ediciones Universitarias de Valparaíso, 1977.
———. *New Islands and Other Stories*. Translation by Richard and Lucía Cunningham. Prologue by Jorge Luis Borges. New York: Farrar, Straus, Giroux, 1982.
———. *La última niebla*. Buenos Aires: Editorial Andina, 1973.
Bonk, Ecke. *Marcel Duchamp: The Box in a Valise*. Translation by David Britt. New York: Rizzoli, 1989.
Borges, Jorge Luis. *El aleph*. Buenos Aires: Translation by Norman Thomas di Giovanni, in collaboration with the author, *The Aleph and Other Stories*. New York: E. P. Dutton, 1970.
———. *Ficciones*. New York: Grove Press, 1962.
———. *El informe de Brodie*. Translation by Anthony Kerrigan et al., *Dr. Brodie's Report*. New York: Bantam, 1973. Buenos Aires: Emecé, 1970.
———. *Libro de sueños*. Buenos Aires: Torres Agüero Editor, 1976.
———. *Obras completas*. Buenos Aires: Emecé, 1974, 1989.
———. *Obras completas en colaboración*. Buenos Aires: Emecé, 1979; Madrid: Siruela, 1989.
———. *A Personal Anthology*. New York: Grove Press, 1967.
Borges, Jorge Luis and Adolfo Bioy Casares. *Libro del cielo y del infierno*. Barcelona: EDHASA, 1971.
Borges, Jorge Luis con Margarita Guerrero. *El libro de los seres*. Buenos Aires: Editorial Kier, 1967. Translated by Norman Thomas di Giovanni, *The Book of Imaginary Beings*. New York: E. P. Dutton, 1970.
Borinsky, Alicia. *Figuras furiosas*. Paris: Revista Rio de la Plata, 1985.
———. *Macedonio Fernández y la teoría crítica: Una evaluación*. Buenos Aires: Editorial Corregidor, 1987.
———. "*Plan de evasión* de Adolfo Bioy Casares: La representación de la representación." In Donald Yates, ed., *Otros mundos, otros fuegos: Fantasía y realismo mágico en Iberoamérica*. East Lansing: Michigan State University, Latin American Studies Center, 1975.
Breton, André. *Second manifesté du surréalisme*. Paris: Sagittaire, 1929.
Cabrera Infante, Guillermo. "Manuel Puig." *El País*, July 24, 1990.
Canetti, Elias. *Ear Witness: Fifty Characters*. Translation by Joachim Neugroschel. New York: Farrar, Straus, Giroux, 1986.
Canto, Estela. *Borges a contraluz*. Espasa Calpe, 1989.
Carpentier, Alejo. *El recurso del metodo*. Buenos Aires: Siglo XXI, 1974.
Cortázar, Julio. *Deshoras*. México: Editorial Nueva Imagen, 1983.
———. *Final de juego*. Buenos Aires: Sudamericana, 1974; Madrid: Ediciones Alfaguara, 1982. Translation by Paul Blackburn, *End of the Game and Other Stories*. New York: Harper and Row, 1978.
———. *Historias de cronopios y de famas*. Buenos Aires: Ediciones Minotauro, 1962.
———. *Rayuela*. Buenos Aires: Editorial Sudamericana, 1963. Translation by Gregory Rabassa, *Hopscotch*. New York: Avon, 1975; Pantheon, 1987. Critical edition edited by Julio Ortega and Saúl Yurkievich. Madrid: CSIC, 1991.
———. *62, Modelo para armar*. Buenos Aires: Editorial Sudamericana, 1968. Translation by Gregory Rabassa, *62: A Model Kit*. New York: Random House, 1972.
———. *Ultimo round*. Madrid: Siglo XXI, 1967.
———. *La vuelta al día en ochenta mundos*. México: Siglo XXI, 1967.

———. *Queremos tanto a Glenda.* México: Nueva Imagen, 1980. Translation by Gregory Rabassa. *We Love Glenda So Much and Other Tales.* New York: Knopf, 1983.
Cortázar, Julio and Carol Dunlop. *Los autonautas de la cosmopista: Un viaje atemporal Paris-Marsella.* Barcelona: Muchnik Editores, 1986.
Cúneo, Dardo. *El romanticismo político: Leopoldo Lugones, Roberto J. Payró, José Ingenieros, Macedonio Fernández, Manuel Ugarte, Alberto Gerchunoff.* Buenos Aires: Editorial Transición, 1955.
Derrida, Jacques. *La vérité en peinture.* Paris: Flammarion, 1978.
Donoso, José. *Casa de campo.* Madrid: Seix Barral, 1978. Translation by David Pritchard with Suzanne Jill Levine, *A House in the Country.* New York: Vintage, 1984.
———. *Cuatro para Delfina.* Barcelona: Seix Barral, 1982.
———. *La desesperanza.* Barcelona: Seix Barral, 1986. Translation by Alfred J. MacAdam, *Curfew.* New York: Weidenfeld and Nicolson, 1988.
———. *El obsceno párajo de la noche.* Madrid: Seix Barral, 1970. Translation by Hardie St. Martin and Leonard Mades, *The Obscene Bird of Night.* New York: Knopf, 1973.
———. *La misteriosa desaparición de la marquesita de Loria.* Barcelona: Seix Barral, 1981.
———. *Tres novelitas burguesas.* Barcelona: Seix Barral, 1973. Translation by Andrée Conrad, *Sacred Families.* New York: Knopf, 1977.
Duras, Marguerite. *Le ravissement de Lol V. Stein.* Paris: Gallimard, 1964.
Fernández, Macedonio. *Adriana Buenos Aires: Última novela mala.* Buenos Aires: Editorial Corregidor, 1974.
———. *Epistolario.* Edited with notes by Alicia Borinsky. Buenos Aires: Editorial Corregidor, 1991.
———. *Macedonio: Selected Writings in Translation.* Edited by Jo Anne Engelbert. Fort Worth, TX: Latitudes Press, 1984.
———. *Museo de la novela de la Eterna: Primera novela buena.* Buenos Aires: Centro Editor de América Latina, 1967; Editorial Corregidor, 1975.
———. *No toda es vigilia la de los ojos abiertos y otros escritos metafísicos.* Buenos Aires: Editorial Corregidor, 1967, 1990.
———. *Papeles de recienvenido y continuación de la nada.* Prologue by Ramón Gómez de la Serna. Buenos Aires: Losada, 1944; Centro Editor de América Latina, 1966; Editorial Corregidor, 1989.
———. "Para una teoría de la Humorística." In Macedonio Fernández, *Papeles de recienvenido.*
———. *Poemas.* México: Editorial Guarania, 1953.
Ferrari, Osvaldo and Jorge Luis Borges. *Diálogos últimos.* Barcelona: Seix Barral, 1992.
Foster, Hannah W. *The Coquette, or, The History of Eliza Wharton: A Novel, Founded on Fact, by a Lady of Massachusetts.* 1811. New York: Oxford University Press, 1986.
Foucault, Michel. *Les mots et les choses: Une archéologie des sciences humaines.* Paris: Gallimard, 1966.
Fuentes, Carlos. *Aura.* México: Era, 1962; Durham, Engl.: University of Durham, 1986.
García, Germán Leopoldo, ed. *Jorge Luis Borges, Arturo Jauretche y otros hablan de Macedonio Fernández.* Buenos Aires: Carlos Pérez Editor, 1969.
García Márquez, Gabriel. *El amor en los tiempos del cólera.* Barcelona: Bruguera,

1985. Translation by Edith Grossman, *Love in the Time of Cholera.* London: Penguin, 1988.

———. *La aventura de Miguel Littín clandestino en Chile.* Buenos Aires: Editorial Sudamericana, 1986.

———. *Cien años de soledad.* Buenos Aires: Editorial Sudamericana, 1967. Translation by Gregory Rabassa, *One Hundred Years of Solitude.* New York: Harper and Row, 1970; reprint Avon, 1974.

———. *Crónica de una muerte anunciada.* Bogotá: Editorial La Oveja Negra, 1981. Translation by Gregory Rabassa, *Chronicle of a Death Foretold.* New York: Knopf, 1983.

———. *El general en su laberinto.* Madrid: Mondadori, 1989. Translation by Edith Grossman, *The General in His Labyrinth.* New York: Knopf, 1990.

———. *La incréible y triste historia de la cándida Eréndira y de su abuela desalmada: Siete cuentos.* Madrid: Mondadori, 1972, 1987. Translation by Gregory Rabassa, *Innocent Erendira and Other Stories.* New York: Harper and Row, 1978.

———. *El otoño del patriarca.* Buenos Aires: Editorial Sudamericana, 1975. Translation by Gregory Rabassa, *The Autumn of the Patriarch.* New York: Avon, 1977.

Genette, Gerard. "L'utopie littéraire." In Genette, *Figures, essaies.* Paris: Éditions du Seuil, 1966.

Giacoman, Helmy F., ed. *Homenaje a Gabriel García Márquez.* Long Island City, NY: Las Américas, 1972.

Goloboff, Gerardo Mario. *Leer Borges.* Buenos Aires: Huemul, 1978.

González Bermejo, Ernesto. "Ahora doscientos años de soledad." *Triunfo* 441 (1970): 12–18.

Gooding, Mel. *Surrealist Games.* Boston: Shambhala Redstone Editions, 1993.

Green, James R. "*El beso de la mujer araña*: Sexual Repression and Textual Repression." In *La Chispa 81: Selected Proceedings of the Louisiana Conference on Hispanic Languages and Literatures,* pp. 131–39. New Orleans: Tulane University, 1981.

Gutiérrez Mouat, Ricardo. *El espacio de la crítica: Estudios de literatura chilena moderna.* Madrid: Orígenes, 1989.

Hancock, Joel. "Gabriel García Márquez's Erendira and the Brothers Grimm." *Studies in Twentieth Century Literature* 3, 1 (1978): 45–52.

Hidalgo, Alberto, Macedonio Fernández, Vicente Huidobro, Jorge Luis Borges, and others. *Indice de la nueva poesía americana.* México and Buenos Aires: Sociedad de Publicaciones El Inca, 1926.

Higonnet, Margaret. "Speaking Silences: Women's Suicide." In Susan Suleiman, ed., *The Female Body in Western Culture.* Cambridge, MA: Harvard University Press, 1986.

Hoffmann, E. T. A. *Tales.* Translation by L. J. Kent and E. C. Knight. Edited by Victor Lange. New York: Continuum, 1982.

Huidobro, Vicente. "Manifestos." In *Obras completas.* Volume 1. Santiago: Editorial Zig Zag, 1976.

Irby, James. "Borges, Carriego y el arrabal." In Jaime Alazraki, ed., *Jorge Luis Borges.* Madrid: Taurus, 1976.

Irwin, John. "The Journey to the South: Poe, Borges and Faulkner." *Virginia Quarterly Review* 67, 3 (Summer 1991): 417–31.

Jitrik, Noé. *Escritores argentinos: Dependencia o libertad.* Buenos Aires: Ediciones del Candil, 1967.

———. "Estructura y significado en *Ficciones* de Jorge Luis Borges." In Juan Fló, ed., *Contra Borges.* Buenos Aires: Galerna, 1978.

Kadir, Djelal. "The Architectonic Principle of *Cien años de soledad* and the Vichian Theory of History." *Kentucky Romance Quarterly* 24, 3 (1977): 251–61.
Kafka, Franz. "Dearest Father" (1919), as quoted by Borges, in Jorge Luis Borges, *The Book of Imaginary Beings*, p. 26. New York: E. P. Dutton, 1970.
Kerr, Lucille. *Suspended Fictions: Reading Novels by Manuel Puig.* Urbana: University of Illinois Press, 1987.
Lagos-Pope, María Inés. "Silencio y rebeldía: Hacia una valoración de María Luisa Bombal dentro la tradición de la escritura femenina." In M. Agosín, E. Gascón-Vera, and Joy Renjilian Burgy, eds., *Maria Luisa Bombal: Apreciaciones críticas.* Tempe, AZ: Bilingual Press, 1987.
Leduc, Violette. *L'affamée.* Paris: Gallimard, 1948, 1972.
Levine, Suzanne Jill. "Adolfo Bioy Casares y Jorge Luis Borges: La utopía como texto." *Revista Iberoamericana* 43 (July–December 1977): 415–32.
———. *Guía de Adolfo Bioy Casares.* Madrid: Fundamentos, 1982.
Lezama Lima, José. "Acerca de *Rayuela.*" *Revista de Casa de las Américas* 7, 49 (July–August 1968): 68. (Havana)
Lindstrom, Naomi. "El discurso de *La amortajada:* Convención burguesa vs. conciencia cuestionadora." In M. Agosín, E. Gascón-Vera, and Joy Renjilian Burgy, eds., *María Luisa Bombal: Apreciaciones críticas*, pp. 147–61. Tempe, AZ: Bilingual Press, 1987.
———. *Macedonio Fernández.* Lincoln, NB: Society of Spanish and Spanish-American Studies, 1981.
Lispector, Clarice. *Laços de Familia.* Río: Editôra do Autor, 1960. Translation by Giovanni Pontiero, *Family Ties.* Austin: University of Texas Press, 1972.
Luchting, Wolfgang A. "Gabriel García Márquez: The Boom and the Wimper." *Books Abroad* 44 (Winter 1970): 26–30.
MacAdam, Alfred J. *El individuo y el otro: Crítica a los cuentos de Julio Cortázar.* Buenos Aires: Librería, 1971.
Marechal, Leopoldo. *Adán Buenosayres.* Buenos Aires: Editorial Sudamericana, 1966.
Martino, Daniel, ed. *ABC de Adolfo Bioy Casares: Reflexiones y observaciones tomadas de su obra.* Alcalá de Henares: Ediciones de la Universidad, 1991.
Masiello, Francine. "Jailhouse Flicks: Projections by Manuel Puig." *Symposium* 32 (Spring 1978): 15–25.
Masson, André. Illustration for *Justine. Obliques*, no. 12–13, p. 14. Éditions Borderie, 1977.
Mastretta, Angeles. *Mujeres de ojos grandes.* Buenos Aires: Planeta Sur, 1992.
McGuirk, Bernard, and Richard Cardwell. *Gabriel García Márquez: New Readings.* Cambridge: Cambridge University Press, 1987.
Mehlman, Jeffrey. "Pierre Menard, Author of *Don Quixote* Again." *L'esprit créateur* 22, 4 (Winter 1983): 22–37.
Mendoza, Plinio Apuleyo. *El olor de la guayaba.* Barcelona: Bruguera, 1982.
Merrim, Stephanie. "For a New (Psychological) Novel in the Works of Manuel Puig." *Novel* 17 (Winter 1984): 141–57.
Mignolo, Walter. "Emergencia, espacio 'mundos posibles': La propuestas epistemológicas de Jorge Luis Borges." *Revista Iberoamericana* 100–101 (1967): 337–56.
Molloy, Sylvia. *Las letras de Borges.* Buenos Aires: Editorial Sudamericana, 1979.
Nabokov, Vladimir. *Lectures on Don Quixote.* New York: Harcourt Brace Jovanovich, 1983.
———. *Strong Opinions.* New York: McGraw-Hill, 1973.

Naville, Pierre. *Le temps du surréel.* Paris: Galilée, 1977.
Nogue, Paul. "La vision dejouée." *Le Surréalisme au service de la Révolution,* p. 26. Paris: Éditions des Cahiers Libres, May 1933. Reprinted in *Le Surréalisme au service de la Révolution.* Paris: Jean-Michel Place, 1975.
Onetti, Juan Carlos. *Cuentos secretos: Periquitá el Aguador y otras máscaras.* Montevideo: Marcha, 1986.
———. *Dejemos hablar al viento.* 3rd ed. Barcelona: Bruguera, 1979.
———. *La muerte y la niña.* Buenos Aires: Editorial Corregidor, 1973.
———. *Obras completas.* Madrid: Aguilar, 1970.
———. *Tan triste como ella y otros cuentos.* Barcelona: Lumen, 1976.
Ortega, Julio. "Borges y la cultura hispanoamericana." *Revista Iberoamericana* 100–101 (1967): 257–68.
———. "Gabriel García Márquez: *Cien años de soledad.*" In *La contemplación y la fiesta: Ensayos sobre la nueva novela latinoamericana.* Lima: Editorial Universitaria, 1968.
Oviedo, José Miguel. "Angeles abominables: Las mujeres en las historias fantásticas de Bioy Casares." In Oviedo, *Escrito al margen.* Bogotá: Procultura, 1982.
———. "La aventura de un fotógrafo en La Plata." *Vuelta* 120 (November 1986): 58–60.
Pacheco, José Emilio. *El principio del placer.* México: Joaquín Mortiz, 1972.
Palau de Nemes, Graciela. "Gabriel García Márquez: *El otoño del patriarca.*" *Hispamérica* 4, 11–12 (1975): 172–83.
Palencia Roth, Michael. *Gabriel García Márquez: La linéa, el círculo y las metamorfosis del mito.* Madrid: Gredos, 1983.
Peignot, Jerome and the group Change, eds. *Écrits de Laure.* Paris: Pauvert, 1977.
Pellón, Gustavo. "Manuel Puig's Contradictory Strategy: Kitsch Paradigms Versus Paradigmatic Strategies in *El beso de la mujer araña* and *Pubis angelical.*" *Symposium* 36 (1983): 186–201.
Penuel, A. M. "The Sleep of Vital Reason in García Márquez's *Crónica de una muerte anunciada.*" *Hispania* 68 (December 1985): 753–66.
Peret, Benjamin. "Ces animaux de la famille." *Le Surréalisme au service de la Révolution.* Paris: Gallimard, March 1, 1926. Reprinted in *Le Surréalisme au service de la Révolution.* Paris: Jean-Michel Place, 1976.
Pezzoni, Enrique. "Bioy Casares: Adversos milagros." In Pezzoni, *El escritor y su voces,* pp. 237–45. Buenos Aires: Editorial Sudamericana, 1986.
Picón Garfield, Evelyn. *Cortázar por Cortázar.* Veracruz, Mexico: Universidad Veracruzana, 1978.
Pizarnik, Alejandra. *Obras completas.* Buenos Aires: Editorial Corregidor, 1992.
Puig, Manuel. *El beso de la mujer araña.* Barcelona: Seix Barral, 1979. Translation by Thomas Colchie, *The Kiss of the Spider Woman.* New York: Knopf, 1979.
———. *Boquitas pintadas.* Barcelona: Seix Barral, 1972. Translation by Suzanne Jill Levine, *Heartbreak Tango: A Serial.* New York: E. P. Dutton, 1975.
———. *Cae la noche tropical.* Barcelona: Seix Barral, 1988. Translation by Suzanne Jill Levine, *Tropical Night Falling.* New York: Simon and Schuster, 1991.
———. *Maldición eterna a quien lea estas páginas.* Barcelona: Seix Barral, 1980.
———. *Pubis angelical.* Barcelona: Seix Barral, 1979. Translation by Elena Brunet, *Pubis Angelical: A Novel.* New York: Random House, 1986.

---. *Sangre de amor correspondido.* Barcelona: Seix Barral, 1982. Translation by Jan L. Grayson, *Blood of Requited Love.* New York: Vintage, 1984.
---. *La traición de Rita Hayworth.* Buenos Aires: Editorial Jorge Alvarez, 1968. Translation by Suzanne Jill Levine, *Betrayed by Rita Hayworth.* New York: E. P. Dutton, 1971.
Rama, Angel. "Un patriarca en la remozada galería de dictadores." *Eco* 29, 178 (1975): 408–43.
Rentería Mantilla, Alfonso, ed. *García Márquez habla de García Márquez: 33 reportajes.* Bogotá: Rentería, 1979.
Roa Bastos, Augusto. *Yo, el supremo.* Buenos Aires: Siglo XXI, 1975. Translation by Helen Lane, *I, the Supreme.* New York: Knopf, 1986.
Robbe-Grillet, Alain. "Adolfo Bioy Casares: *L'invention de Morel.*" *Critique* 69 (February 1963).
Rodríguez Luis, Julio. "*Boquitas pintadas*: Folletín unanimista?" *Sin nombre* 5, 1 (1974): 50–56.
Rodríguez Monegal, Emir. "Borges y la 'Nouvelle Critique.'" In Jaime Alazraki, ed., *Jorge Luis Borges,* pp. 267–87. Madrid: Taurus, 1976.
---. *Jorge Luis Borges: A Literary Biography.* New York: E. P. Dutton, 1978.
---. "*One Hundred Years of Solitude,* the Last Three Pages." *Books Abroad* 47 (1973): 485–89.
Schmucler, Héctor. "*Rayuela*: Judicio a la literatura." *Pasado y presente* (April–September 1965): 29–45. (Córdoba, Argentina)
Senda Nueva Ediciones. *Las desterradas del paraíso: Protagonistas en María Luisa Bombal.* New York: Senda Nueva Ediciones, 1983.
Singer, Isaac Bashevis. *Shosha.* New York: Avon, 1982.
Sosnowski, Saúl. *Borges y la Cábala: La búsqueda del verbo.* Buenos Aires: Hispamérica, 1976.
Sturrock, John. "Odium Theologicum." In Harold Bloom, ed., *Jorge Luis Borges.* New York: Chelsea House, 1986.
Sucre, Guillermo. *Borges, el poeta.* México: UNAM, 1967.
Suleiman, Susan. *Subversive Intent: Gender, Politics and the Avant-Garde.* Cambridge, MA: Harvard University Press, 1990.
Swanson, Philip. "Structure and Meaning in *La misteriosa desaparición de la marquesita de Loria.*" *Bulletin of Hispanic Studies* 3 (July 1986): 247–56.
Tamargo, Maribel. *La narrativa de Bioy Casares: El texto como escritura-lectura.* Madrid: Playor, 1983.
Valdivieso, Mercedes. "Social Denunciation in the Language of 'El Arbol' by María Luisa Bombal." *Latin American Literary Review* 4, 9 (1976): 70–77.
Vargas Llosa, Mario. *Gabriel García Márquez: Historia de un deicidio.* Barcelona: Seix Barral, 1971.
---. "García Márquez: From Aracataca to Macondo." *Review* 70 (1971): 129–42.
von Hagen, Victor W. *The Four Seasons of Manuela.* London: J. M. Dent and Sons, 1952.
Williams, Raymond L. "The Dynamic Structure of García Márquez's *El otoño del patriarca.*" *Symposium* 32 (Spring 1978): 56–75.
Yurkievich, Saúl. *Fundadores de la nueva poesía latinoamericana.* Barcelona: Seix Barral, 1971.
---. *Julio Cortázar: Al calor de tu sombra.* Buenos Aires: Legasa, 1987.
---. "La pujanza insumisa." In Julio Cortázar, *Rayuela,* critical edition by Julio Ortega and Saúl Yurkievich, pp. 661–74. Madrid: CSIS, 1991.

Index

Achúgar, Hugo, 130.
Agosín, Marjorie, 116.
Alazraki, Jaime, 32, 33.
Alexandrian, Sarane, 72.
Andreu, Jean, 72.
Arlt, Roberto, 53.

Bacarisse, Pamela, 102.
Barrenechea, Ana María, 33.
Barth, John, 130.
Bashevis Singer, Isaac, 51.
Bastos, María Luisa, 116.
Bathory, Erzébet, 72.
Baudelaire, Charles, 130–31.
Bellmer, Hans, 72
Bernárdez, Francisco Luis, 4.
Bioy Casares, Adolfo, vii, xiii, 33, 73–87, 102, 127, 133.
Blanchot, Maurice, 5.
Blanqui, Louis Auguste, 78, 86.
Bloom, Harold, 32.
Bolívar, Simón, 23–24, 44.
Bombal, María Luisa, xii, xiii, 104–107, 133.
Bonk, Ecke, 71.
Borges, Jorge Luis, xi–xiv, 10, 11, 15, 17–34, 37, 45, 48, 53, 58, 73, 84–86, 101, 115, 132.
Breton, André, 130.
Britt, David, 71.
Brunet, Elena, 103.
Bruto, César, 59, 62–63.

Cabrera Infante, Guillermo, 100, 103.
Calderón de la Barca, Pedro, 9.
Canetti, Elias, 88, 102.

Canto, Estela, 33.
Cardwell, Richard, 50.
Carpentier, Alejo, 51.
Céline, Louis-Ferdinand, 21–22, 71.
Cervantes, Miguel de, 8, 19–21, 23, 32, 50.
Conrad, Andrée, 131.
Cortázar, Julio, xii, 6, 11, 14, 16, 36, 50, 53–74, 85, 129, 132–133.
Cúneo, Dardo, 15.

Dabove, César, 1.
Dabove, Santiago, 1.
Darío, Rubén, 130.
Daudet, Leon, 22.
Davis, Bette, 91.
Derrida, Jacques, xiv, 73–74, 86.
Dietrich, Marlene, 91.
Donoso, José, xii–xiii, 71, 118–131, 133.
Duchamp, Marcel, 71.
Duras, Marguerite, 116.

Eluard, Paul, 64.
Engelbert, Jo Anne, 15.

Fenichel, Otto, 93.
Fernández, Macedonio, xi–xiv, 1–16, 27, 29, 54, 56, 72, 132–133.
Ferrari, Osvaldo, 33.
Fló, Juan, 32.
Foster, Hannah W., 88, 102.
Foucault, Michel, 33.

García Márquez, Gabriel, xii, 34–52, 118, 132.
García, Germán Leopoldo, 16.

Gascón-Vera, Elena, 116.
Genette, Gerard, 33.
Gerchunoff, Alberto, 15.
Giacoman, Helmy, 50.
Goloboff, Gerardo Mario, 33.
Gómez de la Serna, Ramón, xi, xiv, 9, 16.
Góngora, Luis de, 22.
González Bermejo, Ernesto, 50.
Gooding, Mel, 72.
Gourmont, Remy de, 31
Green, Ray, 102.
Grossman, Edith, 52.

Hagen, Victor W. von, 51.
Hernández, Felisberto, 54.
Hidalgo, Alberto, 1, 4, 15.
Higonnet, Margaret, 116.
Hoffmann, E. T. A., 76, 86, 104, 115.
Huidobro, Vicente, 7, 12, 16, 131.

Ingenieros, José, 15.
Irby, James, 32.
Irwin, John, 32.

Jarry, Alfred, 54.
Jauretche, Arturo, 16.
Jitrik, Noé, 32.
Joyce, James, 21.

Kadir, Djelal, 50.
Kafka, Franz, 17–19, 28, 31.
Kaiser, Ernst, 31.
Kent, L. J., 86.
Kerr, Lucille, 102.
Knight, E. C., 86.

Lacan, Jacques, 117.
Lagos-Pope, María Inés, 116.
Lange, Victor, 86.
Lautréamont, Comte de, 54.
Leduc, Violette, 116.
Levine, Suzanne Jill, 86, 87, 102, 130.
Lezama Lima, José, 54, 70.
Lindstrom, Naomi, 16, 116.
Lispector, Clarice, 51.
Lugones, Leopoldo, 15.

MacAdam, Alfred J., 71, 131.
Manzi, Homero, 95–96.
Marechal, Leopoldo, 13, 16.
Martini, Abad, 59.

Martino, Daniel, 86.
Masiello, Francine, 102.
Masson, André, 70.
Mastretta, Angeles, 103.
McGuirk, Bernard, 50.
Mehlman, Jeffrey, 31.
Mendoza, Plinio Apuleyo, 50.
Merrim, Stephanie, 102.
Mignolo, Walter, 32.
Molloy, Sylvia, 31
Monroe, Marilyn, 101.

Nabokov, Vladimir, 32–33.
Naville, Pierre, 70
Nouge, Paul, 71.

Obieta, Adolfo de, xiii, 1, 15.
Onetti, Juan Carlos, 73, 86.
Ortega, Julio, 32, 50.
Oviedo, José Miguel, 87.

Pacheco, José Emilio, 102–3.
Palau de Nemes, Graciela, 51.
Palencia Roth, Michael, 51.
Payró, Roberto, 15.
Paz, Octavio, 54–55.
Peignot, Jerome, 117.
Pellón, Gustavo, 102.
Penrose, Valentine, 72.
Penuel, A. M., 51.
Peret, Benjamin, 70.
Pérez Galdós, Benito, 60.
Pezzoni, Enrique, 87.
Picón-Garfield, Evelyn, 53, 70.
Pizarnik, Alejandra, 72, 116.
Poe, Edgar Alan, 9, 73.
Puig, Manuel, xii, xiii, 88–103, 129, 133.

Quevedo, Francisco de, 8, 22, 32.

Rabassa, Gregory, 50–51, 71–72.
Rais, Gilles de, 72.
Rama, Angel, 51.
Rentería Mantilla, Alfonso, 50.
Renzilian Burgy, Joy, 116.
Roa Bastos, Augusto, 51.
Robbe-Grillet, Alain, 86.
Rodríguez Larreta, Enrique, 22, 32.
Rodríguez Monegal, Emir, 31, 32, 33, 50.
Rodríguez Luis, Julio, 102.

Rossetti, Dante Gabriel, 78.
Rybalka, Michel, 130.

Sade, Donatien, Marquis de, 71.
Saint-Saëns, Charles Camille, 57.
San Martín, José de, 23–25.
Sánchez, Manuela, 51.
Santiago, Hugo, 86.
Scalabrini Ortiz, Raúl, 4.
Schmucler, Héctor, 70.
Sosnowski, Saúl, 33.
Spinoza, Baruch, 60.
Stroheim, Erich von, 74.
Sturrock, John, 31–32.
Sucre, Guillermo, 33.

Suleiman, Susan, 116–117.
Swanson, Philip, 131.

Tamargo, Maribel, 86.
Turner, Lana, 100.

Ugarte, Manuel, 15.

Valdivieso, Mercedes, 116.
Valéry, Paul, 118.
Vargas Llosa, Mario, 35–36, 50.

Wilkins, Eithne, 31.
Williams, Raymond, 51.

Yates, Donald, 86.
Yurkievich, Saúl, 32, 71.

Permission is acknowledged to reprint material from the following sources:

Adolfo Bioy Casares, *The Invention of Morel and Other Stories*, translated by Ruth L. C. Simms. Translation copyright © 1964 by the University of Texas Press. Reprinted by permission of the University of Texas Press.

Adolfo Bioy Casares, *Asleep in the Sun*, translated by Suzanne Jill Levine. Copyright © 1940 by Adolfo Bioy Casares, translation copyright © 1978 by Suzanne Jill Levine. Reprinted by permission of Emecé and Persea Books, Inc.

María Luisa Bombal, *New Islands and Other Stories*, translated by Richard and Lucia Cunningham. Copyright © 1982 by Farrar, Straus & Giroux, Inc. Reprinted by permission of Farrar, Straus & Giroux, Inc.

Jorge Luis Borges, "Pierre Menard, Author of *Don Quixote*." Translation copyright © 1962 by Grove Press, Inc. Reprinted by permission of Grove Press, Inc.

Jorge Luis Borges, "The Sandman." Translation copyright © 1967 by Grove Press, Inc. Reprinted by permission of Grove Press, Inc.

Elias Canetti, *Ear Witness: Fifty Characters*, translated by Joachim Neugroschel, translation copyright © 1986 by Continuum Publishing Company. Reprinted by permission of Continuum Publishing Company.

Julio Cortázar, *62: A Model Kit*, translated by Gregory Rabassa. Copyright © 1968 by Julio Cortazar. Translation copyright © 1972 by Gregory Rabassa. Reprinted by permission of Editorial Sudamericana and Random House Publishers, Inc.

José Donoso, *A House in the Country*, translated by Suzanne Jill Levine. Copyright © 1978 by José Donoso, translation copyright © by Suzanne Jill Levine. Reprinted by permission of Editorial Seix Barral and Alfred A. Knopf, Inc.

José Donoso, *La misteriosa desaparicion de la marquesita de Loria*. Copyright © 1981 by José Donoso. Reprinted by permission of Editorial Seix Barral.

Gabriel García Márquez, *One Hundred Years of Solitude*, translated by Gregory Rabassa. Copyright © 1967 by Gabriel García Márquez, translation copyright © 1970 by Harper & Row, Publishers, Inc. Reprinted by permission of Editorial Sudamericana and HarperCollins Publishers, Inc.

Gabriel García Márquez, *Innocent Erendira and Other Stories*, translated by Gregory Rabassa. Copyright © 1973 by Gabriel García Márquez, translation copyright © 1978 by Harper & Row, Publishers, Inc. Reprinted by permission of Mondadori and HarperCollins Publishers, Inc.

Gabriel García Márquez, *Love in the Time of Cholera*, translated by Edith Grossman. Copyright © 1985 by Gabriel Garcia Marquez, translation copyright © 1988 by Harper & Row, Inc. Reprinted by permission of Brugeira and HarperCollins Publishers, Inc.

Manuel Puig, *Pubis Angelical: A Novel*, translated by Elena Brunet. Copyright © 1979 by Manuel Puig, translation copyright © 1986 by Elena Brunet. Reprinted by permission of Seix Barral and Alfred A. Knopf, Inc.

Manuel Puig, *Betrayed by Rita Haworth*, translated by Suzanne Jill Levine. Copyright © 1968 by Manuel Puig, translation copyright © 1971 by E. P. Dutton & Co., Inc. Reprinted by permission of Editorial Jorge Alvarez and Penguin Books USA, Inc.

Manuel Puig, *Kiss of the Spider Woman*, translated by Thomas Colchie. Copyright © 1979 by Manuel Puig, translation copyright © 1979 by Alfred A. Knopf, Inc. Reprinted by permission of Editorial Seix Barral and Alfred A. Knopf, Inc.

Penn Studies in Contemporary American Fiction
A Series Edited by Emory Elliott, University of California at Riverside

Alicia Borinsky. *Theoretical Fables: The Pedagogical Dream in Contemporary Latin-American Fiction.* 1993
Silvio Gaggi. *Modern/Postmodern: A Study in Twentieth-Century Arts and Ideas.* 1989
John Johnston. *Carnival of Repetition: Gaddis's* The Recognitions *and Postmodern Theory.* 1990
Paul Maltby. *Dissident Postmodernists: Barthelme, Coover, Pynchon.* 1991
Ellen Pifer. *Saul Bellow Against the Grain.* 1990
Arthur M. Saltzman. *Designs of Darkness in Contemporary American Fiction.* 1990
Brian Stonehill. *The Self-Conscious Novel: Artifice in Fiction from Joyce to Pynchon.* 1988
Patricia Tobin. *John Barth and the Anxiety of Continuance.* 1992
Alan Wilde. *Middle Grounds: Studies in Contemporary American Fiction.* 1987

This book was set in Baskerville and Eras typefaces. Baskerville was designed by John Baskerville at his private press in Birmingham, England, in the eighteenth century. The first typeface to depart from oldstyle typeface design, Baskerville has more variation between thick and thin strokes. In an effort to insure that the thick and thin strokes of his typeface reproduced well on paper, John Baskerville developed the first wove paper, the surface of which was much smoother than the laid paper of the time. The development of wove paper was partly responsible for the introduction of typefaces classified as modern, which have even more contrast between thick and thin strokes.

Eras was designed in 1969 by Studio Hollenstein in Paris for the Wagner Typefoundry. A contemporary script-like version of a sans-serif typeface, the letters of Eras have a monotone stroke and are slightly inclined.

Printed on acid-free paper.